The Craig; Rainbow in my Fears

Life Story & Psychiatric Tales

Rod Maclean

authorHOUSE®

AuthorHouse™ UK Ltd.
500 Avebury Boulevard
Central Milton Keynes, MK9 2BE
www.authorhouse.co.uk
Phone: 08001974150

First published by AuthorHouse 4/12/2010

ISBN: 978-1-4490-8799-9 (sc)

This book is printed on acid-free paper.

Contents

Introduction.

Achilles clinic; Counselling services now available for individuals, groups and employee assistance programs.
Brief therapy for good results and cost effectiveness.
Registered psychotherapist/hypnotherapist and British Association counseller.

The building stared down malignantly over the Caledonian Canal, the river Ness and onto the capital of the Highlands, Inverness. Evil was personified by the evening shadow that crawled down the gradual slope, threatening to engulf the town and the graveyard, where souls would moan and try to shrug of the horrors of darkness. Sitting at the top of a huge hill, the conventional sandstone construction made it look like a workhouse, from the Victorian era. The skyline showed the odd spire, casticulations and towers, what did they do there? Why did people avoid questions about the place? When some brave souls took a short cut through the grounds at night, they swore they heard terrifying screams and devils laughter.

Monks were rumoured to have built the place many years before. This idea was reinforced by the huge dormitory above the main corridor, which resembled a cathedral, with its massive vaulted roof; it was named the Chapels. They were said to have introduced trout to the small loch on the higher west side. The long cellar, underneath the female hospital, was seldom visited after dark, as many of the nurses had sworn they had seen the 'White Lady' hovering there! In fact, it was built in the late nineteenth century. A public meeting of the Parochial Board announced that the number of lunatics was increasing and a local asylum could save hundreds, due to the board having to send them elsewhere and paying for their maintenance. Sometimes the rumours were more interesting!

The main hospital was 'T' shaped, with the top longer than the leg. This top piece was just over a kilometre long, the male side on the right and the female side to the left. In the middle were the medical records and the doctor's offices; there was also a small medical library. Going down the leg halfway were corridors off to the right and left, leading to male and female wards. Next, came the matrons' and enquires offices. Further down, on the left, was the opening leading to the front entrance. The staff changing rooms and the patients clothing store were further down on the left. At the bottom, the doors opened into the majestic recreation hall. The highly polished pine floor leading the eye up to the stage, where many famous performers did their, voluntary, turns! To the left of the stage was the welfare office, the office for the recreational staff, was situated on the other side.

The spacious grounds around the hospital contained the Physician Superintendents huge mansion, the Sanatorium ward, overlooking the football pitch, Crematorium, Villa ward, Laundry and sewing room adjoining the engineers, joiners and ground staff workshops, behind all this, on the hillside, lay the eighteen hole golf course. The nurses' home also housed the kitchen and dining room for the staff. Between this and the main hospital stood the beautiful church, which the patients had helped to build!

Home Sweet Home.

I was introduced to drunkenness at an early age! My uncle and aunt, the lodger and then my mother all hit the bottle! Mother had been a very proud lady. She had helped her mother and father run their fishmongers, in the market. When they passed on, she took up waitressing. Turned out she was a natural, hardly surprising, black hair, good looking and a trim figure. Sharp as a ninja blade, fluent French and passable Gaelic, all made her the centre of attraction. Eventually, the stress of her brothers, sister and lodgers drinking, coupled with raising my sister and me, drove her to an escape through alcohol.

It would not have been so bad if we had not all lived together in the same house, along with my older sister, cousin, a dog and a cat. Every week, when they were paid, the house would be empty. One at a time, they would saunter in, pleasant and bubbly. My uncle usually came in first and always with the same story. "How are you doing kid? Remind me to take you to that beautiful forest where I once worked with the Forestry. The birds and butterflies, huge birch, spruce and magnificent oak trees, all blending together to protect their wildlife. We'll go there next weekend". Each time I thought, 'Maybe this time it will happen! We can have a picnic in the clearing, watch the splendour all around us, pointing out all the different birds and butterflies, flowers and fungi'. Of course, it never happened, although I clung to the dream, as a child does. That was until he died and another dream lay shattered on the grave of hope! His handsome face was paler than in life and his black hair, flecked with silver, was full and well groomed. No one cried at his funeral!

Aunty Mary was a kind, gentle soul. She was the brainy one of the family, though lacked the motivation to do anything with her gift, except have kids and drink! Her pitch-black hair, accentuated her white, bloated face. She was much too soft to face the reality that her life was in ruins and getting worse! Her 'common law' husband, Bob, was a big man. The hairy chest and arms compensated a receding hairline. Once employed as a prison warder, apparently, he spoilt the prisoners, with food and cigarettes; he soon drank himself into the unemployable! Sober, he was kind and intelligent, in a 'man of the world' sort of way, enjoyed strumming his ukulele or blowing the mouth organ! He became a cruel bully, when he was drunk. Usually I could dodge his flailing arms, but, on the occasions that I tripped up, he would twist my arm up my back and give me a hiding! They both died soon after each other. His long-suffering ulcer finally exploded and Mary simply faded away.

When they were all together in the house, all hell broke loose! First, they would bring up old grievances, then voices would be raised, idle threats were exchanged, then doors would bang and windows were smashed. I always wondered why we bothered to replace the glass; it would just be knocked out by the end of the week?

As my mother worked during the week, I had my dinners at school, when I attended! In the evenings she would usually bring home a piece of chicken, steak or fish from her job at the hotel. The weekends were not so rosy! No school dinners and mother would join her friends after work at the pub! Sometimes, the woman across the road, who was always' boasting about her son being a famous footballer, would take me in for a plate of soup or mince and tatties. The lady next door, Donny's mother, would even, on occasions, give me a meal, in the forlorn hope that I would stop fighting with her son. He seemed such a pompous, arrogant fatty; it was difficult not to pick on him. We latter became good friends, until he became a policeman and we lost touch. Kenny's mother was also kind to me.

After Kenny and I played cowboys and Indians, looked through his vast collection of Superman comics, his mother would call us for dinner. It never entered my silly little mind that I should be grateful for all their generosity and, in later life, would never have the opportunity to show them how much they really meant to me.

Thankfully, in the autumn, in the back garden, our uncared for, apple trees, there were six of them, would bear many apples. Many happy, gutsy, hours were spent climbing all over these trees. In the evening, it was safer to hide in the shadows, at the side of the house, to see what state the family arrived home in. If they were in a foul mood, I would stay where I was or go for long walks until they fell asleep, then sneak into bed, hoping they wouldn't wake up to resume their debate!

To obtain some respite, I joined the Boys Brigade! 'The fighting fifth'! Most nights I would be out at meetings and classes. Anything was better than being at home, Gymnastics, wayfaring, first aid, drums, signalling, education; I had a sore arm with all the badges on my armband. The vaulting horse was great fun, running up at full pelt, banging onto the springboard and leaping over the leather top. Groundwork was my favourite, headsprings, handsprings, and fly-springs, walking round the hall on our hands. The parallel bars were a frightening piece of equipment, the danger of falling between the bars, or slipping off the end, was a nasty thought, even though there were mats on the floor on either side. If there were still noise when I got home, I would go for a long walk until they were asleep. There were many nights when I would walk for hours through, my friend, the pouring rain.

One evening, after our training session at the hall was finished and we were dismissed, Stanley, one of the officers, called me over. 'I wonder if you could help me out'. His tall military bearing, barrel chest and coal black eyes, told me that very few people would refuse him. 'I need a messenger on Saturdays, to deliver my football reports, to the newspaper office, at half time. You will be paid a half crown and get to watch the game free'. I have never enjoyed football, the newspaper office was a three-mile cycle run from the grounds, through the centre of the town and this would be on the busiest day. The chance to earn some cash and work for a reporter, delivering important newsletters, did it for me. 'Thank you for the offer. I would be delighted to accept'.

My friend, Hugh and I lived beside the Gasworks, as his father was an engineer there, we could sneak through the coal yard, ride up and down the lift in the gantry and climb up the side of the gasometer. The workmen tolerated us, even when we took their empty lemonade bottles and cashed them in for fish and chips. It was mandatory, that we each had to stick our fingers into the broken live switch, at the top of the wooden steps, in the garage. we called this 'ticklers, number one'. Other 'ticklers', were jumping of a high wall, into a graveyard and dropping water from the top of the gasometer, onto the head of 'Peg leg', a one legged woman, who would pass on the street below. "Is that the rain about to start?" she would growl, as she pulled up her collar, oblivious of our laughter high above her.

I hated school. So when it was time to go I would develop a bad racking cough or look ill and miserable enough to warrant a day off school. When these ploys were milked dry, I would hide in the huge oak wardrobe, emerging only when it was too late for school. However, that did not always work, for sometimes aunty Mary would take me by the hand and drag me to the classroom, screaming. There is nothing worse than going in late with a lame excuse for the teacher while the class laugh and hiss. At other times the swings at the Maggot Green, would be my destination, ignoring the other kids marching smartly to school, as if it were normal!

After four o-clock, I could go round and join my friends. This was a happy time when we all played together and nothing was a problem. There was Hugh, tall dark and handsome, Billy, a bundle of nerves, though smart and sensitive, his neighbour Koalene, pretty, red haired doll. There were also the three sisters, Marlene, Marjory and Ellen; they had a younger sister who complained bitterly when left out. Hide and seek, sticky cricket, tag, marbles were our favourite games and sometimes we would just chatter among ourselves. As we grew older, had crushes on all the females but were too shy to tell them, fell out and made up again, our interests diversified and we mostly drifted apart. Hugh and I still kept in touch and we occasionally bumped into the sisters at an anniversary or funeral. My 'older' sister finally left home to pursue her lifelong ambition of becoming a nurse.

Sitting on the steps of the football stand, I tried to make sense of the confusion between the players as they looked about for the ball and the conviction of the spectators that the referee was an idiot and the opposing side were hired assassins. My time for the cycle run to the newspaper office and back was gradually getting faster. Sometimes it was necessary, if a special match was being played, to do the trip several times. It was half-time! Taking the rolled sheath of papers from Stanley, I stuck it into my deep jerkin pocket. This was going to be a record time, as I sped through the busy town. I was almost there and my time was good. That itchy feeling of 'wrong' swept over me. What was I sensing? Oh, No! my jacket pocket felt too light. The report was gone! Almost falling off the bike and running into a woman with her shopping, I screeched to a stop. Like a moron, I looked down, hoping it was at my feet. It wasn't! Turning round, I made my way back to the grounds. Eyes staring at the kerbside, the pavement and under cars, I almost ran over half the population. There was no sign of it anywhere!

Walking up to the reporter's office in the stand, my head hanging as Stanley answered my timid knocking. 'Sorry sir, I've lost your report'. To my amazement, he did not swear, kick or slap me. He even failed to raise his voice! 'Ok lad, I will phone the office and let them know what has happened'. My respect for this man shot up a thousand percent. A real gentleman. He returned after a few minutes, no doubt to send me home. 'The office have the report, someone handed it in'. The sun jumped out from behind a stack of clouds and everything was bright and sparkling. Future trips to the printing office would see a huge safety pin fastening the careless pocket!

New Career

Finally, I was released from my wasted years at school, where I constantly played the fool. Other kids tend to ignore you if they think you are even more stupid than they are. I was bullied regularly, called Ginger and Fishface, due to my red hair and my folks working in a fishmongers.

My first job was in a sweet factory. For two years I worked very hard, ate lots of sweets and felt a useful member of the working class. A huge copper pan with a handle at each side was placed over a burner. Water and sugar were melted down, and then glucose was added and heated until the mixture was tested, by putting your hand in cold water, scooping out a handful into the water, if it hardened to a fine crack then it was ready! Butter and salt were added then condensed milk was slowly poured in, again heated to the correct temperature and as it cooled, vanilla essence was added. The gleaming brown, hot syrup was then poured onto a cold table, turned into a cone and feed through a cutting and wrapping machine to appear as silver wrapped toffees! The packers would then weigh and bag them. They were a great bunch, full of fun and pranks. Inevitably, or so it seemed, the business dried up. (Had I eaten all the profits?) Fifteen people, office staff, packers, cleaners, sugar boilers and management were all on the dole.

It was great going up the town during the day, mingling with 'normal' people. Usually at this time of day, I would have been slaving over a boiling pan of syrup. These people were shopping, eating in café's and checking what was on at the cinemas. I would go fishing in the river and canal; I didn't catch much, the odd cuddy and a couple of eels, maybe a trout if it got careless. But then, slowly and insidiously, it dawned on me that maybe this was not normal, maybe I was kidding myself as I ran out of money for the odd coffee and a cigarette. Luckily, I did not like alcohol, for heaven knows what it would have been like trying to satisfy the craving for a drink. Would I have relied on my 'friends' for a drink? Recovering from a hangover and the self-loathing would have left me mortified. Had my family actually done me a favour, by teaching me the perils of alcohol?

Unemployment had finally hit home. My unemployment benefit was cut in half; I became obsessed by worthlessness and guilt, sunshine was merely a reminder of how my life should be. Like forever wearing very dark sunglasses. Applying for dozens of jobs, filling in crap application forms, which would almost certainly fail to impress any perspective employer, somehow increased my inferiority. No 'O'-levels or highers, no office experience, no ambitions, no proper references. No one needed a 'sugar boiler', the truth was, no one needed me!

To my amazement, a few interviews were forthcoming, but then I really blew my chances. Untidy appearance, lack of any preparation, I was a motivational disaster. Usually, I was made to feel honoured, that they would even speak to me. Some of the bosses were very unpleasant and would give me a dressing down for wasting their precious time. Others were more sympathetic and let me down gently. It was now six months since I had worked and the feeling was beyond despair. Then a frightening thing happened; I was offered a job! The prospect was a mixture of pride and disbelief. As a message boy for a garage, I would deliver machine parts all over town in my shiny message bike. When it was quiet, the floor would be brushed, interdepartmental deliveries carried out and tea served to the counter staff. It was a pleasant enough job, with no stress, but after being used to being my own boss and having some 'position', it was a bit of a downer being ordered all over the place by everyone. I soon realized that there was no chance of any promotion. The chap at the parts counter seemed to know everything there was to know about machines. When a mechanic came for a replacement part, he would be advised how to fit it properly, all the washers, nuts, gaskets, oils and tests that may be required. Listening in awe, to all this knowledge, made me realize that there was no way I could ever do his job. My confidence was now a flickering candlelight, just enough to push me onward and upward. The fact is getting a new job is easier if you are already employed.

A multitude of jobs were to follow; Lemonade factory, most of the time was spent uncorking empty bottles so they could be washed and sterilized. They were then lined up on the conveyer belt, to be once again filled with a mixture of water, flavouring, sugar and carbon dioxide gas. Six months later, it was time to discover the Pulp mill, which involved carting huge logs to a grinder, twelve hour shifts of very heavy work and the wages were poor. There were many other jobs, but I could not stick to any of them for more than six months at a time. I enjoyed my work at a furniture shop, as a driver and handyman and the pay was good, for a time I even worked as a 'stock clerk' and that was a buzz; going round the showrooms pricing everything, but then the bloody place went into liquidation! I needed real job security. The fear, of being thrown onto the scrapheap, would always be with me.

My new job was with a locally owned furniture shop. An 'up-market' affair that had been inherited by the son. He was kind and considerate towards me though a shrewd businessman at heart. He would squeeze his huge frame into his Mini Cooper, which he always parked outside his shop and as this was on the main street, would regularly receive a parking ticket. His already red face would go scarlet as he condemned the victimisation by the 'yellow peril'.

In the shop a space, under the stair, was dedicated to a spectacular lighting display. All manner of standard lamps, table lamps, wall fittings, pendant lights, etc, etc, etc, were on show. I was granted free expression, to arrange this playground of light and colour. I was in my element. Then it was onto some long haul deliveries, with the freedom of the open road and a pay rise! But my fear of future unemployment, seeped through me, like a tide of putrification!

My time had come to push my chances to the limit! My good friend and father figure, Dunc Cruick, advised me to apply to the local mental hospital, as an assistant nurse. The only thing that made me even consider this, high office, was because Dunc, had connections through the 'Free Masons' and would provide me with a real reference. In the interim, I had attended night school and was the proud bearer of a mighty, educational accolade, an 'o' level in English, wow!

It was grey and cold, a typical January day. The entrance vestibule was obviously a recent addition. Although they had stuck to the quasie-victorian lines, it stuck out like a granny flat. Before I had walked two paces, a tall, fat, though handsome woman asked if she could have a cigarette, on saying I had none, she looked at me incredulously. I scurried along the imposing grandeur that was the corridor of the psychiatric hospital, to the reception desk. "Matron's office, turn right down the corridor, first on the left". The man at the desk, 'Jinny', was boldly emblazoned on the nametag, fired the directions at me, and then glowered, daring me to ask another stupid question. As I gazed down the immense, gleaming, tiled corridor, several men and women ambled past me and I imagined them suffering from all sorts of insanity. Were they paranoid, demented, homicidal, suicidal, epileptic? My heartbeat scared me, as my eyes darted from face to face, trying to anticipate who would strike first!

Her long silver-blond curls swept down her chubby, cheeky face and draped over her huge breasts. Standing six inches taller than me, she moved incredibly fast for such a big girl. The pain in my privates gave me stomach cramp, as her massive hand closed around them, like a vice. "Any time you need me, baby, just call for Martha". Laughing incongruously, she tiptoed out the door.

I was standing in front of the biggest, thickest door, I had ever seen. My knock sounded feeble. "Come in". I instantly obeyed the command. Two uniformed ladies and a man, in a black suit, nailed me with their penetrating stare. They surely must realize this article before them is just a waste of their precious time. The small, stern looking lady, with the great, frilly white, mausoleum on her head, was obviously the matron. "This is the deputy matron, Ms. Patricksen, and Mr. Mortiman, our head tutor. I am Ms. Smith, the matron". Mr. Mortiman's black piercing eyes, under heavy black eyebrows, looked so wild, I expected him to bellow, as he addressed me. "You mentioned in your application, that you have an O-level in English, a green belt in judo, possess a driving license and have entertained OAPs, in concerts". His voice was melodic and kind. My tongue shrivelled into flypaper. What was the response that I had rehearsed? It had sounded great at home, but now it seemed pathetic. "I have gained a wide experience from the many jobs that I have worked in. (many of which I left dubiously and not always voluntarily.) "This, I believe, has given me the maturity and experience to do a good job in nursing".

They turned to each other, muttering incomprehensibly. This is where I will be told, 'Sling your hook'. 'We will be in touch with you, but don't hold your breath', and that will be the last I will hear from them.

Matron turned to face me, standing erect and proud, in all her five foot of primness. The other two looked on, like sheep at the slaughter. "You will start on Monday, at six-thirty in the morning. Report to the reception desk and ask for the chief male nurse, Mr. Frazier".

I was walking down the brae by the canal, before it dawned on me that I had finally gotten a job that I really wanted to do!

Flyaway Problem

The phone startled me from my thirty-year-old reverie. "Would you be able to take on a case for us? A thirty year old female has a problem sleeping and her marriage is under pressure". I informed them that I would be happy to take on the assignment. "Her name is, Susan Trippe, it's her husband who is the employee of, Morac Electronics, But the contract covers dependants".

She would be allowed six sessions, the usual forms would be sent, confidentiality, information release, work-specific contract and, most important, expenses sheet.

Counselling Consultants Ltd. had taken me on because I was the only person in the area registered with the, British Association for Counselling. I phoned Susan, and arranged her appointment.

She arrived at my house, where the clinic was in an upstairs room, parked her three litre, limited edition Capri at the door and strode confidently into the session. My blood ran cold. A sure sign that the, Sword of Damocles, was due to fall. Was it just nerves?

The first session is mainly concerned with collecting all the personal details, but I wanted to get things moving quickly. There seemed to be an underlying current that needed to be ventilated. The caked make-up symbolized her need to hide behind a mask of normality, but the darting eyes, quivering lips, fidgety hands and feet painted a different picture! As I cut through, her 'many layered' mask, the venom poured out in ever-increasing amounts. In short, her father was a maniac that had beaten the daylights out of her

13

sister, mother and herself since she could remember. The terrible thing was that he then became aroused. Through the crying and screaming, he would enjoy full sexual intercourse with both his daughters.

Even now, when he returned from a business trip, he would beat-up her mother. "She keeps falling down the stairs or running into things". He would say to explain away her bumps and bruises to the doctor. However, even more worrying was the fact that he would, on occasions, baby-sit for her two and three year old daughters!

The presenting problem was her claustrophobia. At night she would wake up terrified, the ceiling and walls pressing down on her chest. Her two children would be standing at the foot of her bed, wakened by her screaming. As Susan yelled at them for daring to waken her, they cowered in the corner. She was frightened of losing control and lashing out at them.

Unfortunately, some people have difficulty accepting that something that happened in our past may affect our future. That is probably because the resulting problems can be so subtle and tangential. As a young child, seeing your parents having sex could not result in you having guilt feelings. Could it? Perhaps you never learnt to swim or simply have no interest in swimming! Could it have anything to do with your mother splashing water in your face while having a bath, when you were a baby! Do you remember choking and crying? A child's imagination is so powerful and ultra real, it can create a lifetime of beliefs! Both good and bad.

So it was to be that Susan resisted any suggestion that her previous experience may be responsible for her present dilemma. Fortunately, insight is not always a prerequisite to resolution of a problem. She was taught a relaxation technique with ego boosting. "You must have a strong character, to have survived up to now". All the positive things in her life were discussed and reinforced. On top of this, suggestions were made, that the deeper part of her mind would now be able to let go the problems and thus create better ways to go forward.

These clients are typically desperate to be in total control and any perceived threat could result in mayhem. Protective layers are installed to avoid becoming aware, or feel the original horrible hurt, pain, fear or vulnerability that caused the cover-up in the first place. All kinds of defence mechanisms can be activated, to guard the door leading to your personal dungeon, where chains rattle, doors creak, spider webs abound and snakes wriggle through the ominous, black waters!

In the middle of the night Susan would phone me with accusations of making her problems worse, causing her to become suicidal and interfering with her mind. When she stopped for breath, I would explain that it had been her decision to come for treatment and these possible reactions, had been explained, she had agreed to every part of it and if she still felt the same in the morning simply phone and cancel her remaining appointments. It was her prerogative. A week later she phoned, thanked me for my help and stated her husband was being transferred to a job in New Mexico and they were all flying out in a week.

When I first started counselling the need to be in charge of the procedure was very important to me. Asking all manner of leading questions, focusing on what I thought was the main problem and then the best solution. Before the second session, I would have a list of possible techniques and outcomes with more leading questions to take my client to a therapeutic conclusion. Looking back, it seems obvious, that the complexed look on the client's face was indicating that what I thought and they thought, were two different things, but at the time, my fear overcame my judgement. Thankfully, I soon realised that the client knew best. It was simply a case of listening to them and helping them to make informed choices. Most people have listened to other people's problems and thought the solution was obvious, but more often than not, the person is too wrapped-up in their emotions to think straight. Maybe that is why it has been said, 'The last thing man will understand is his own mind'!

DAY ONE

The chief male nurse, Mr. Frazier, greeted me with a powerful handshake and as my arm recovered I ran to follow his massive strides along the, seemingly, never-ending corridor. We raced past the door leading to the doctors' offices, on the right the pharmacy, senile ward on the left, insulin ward on the right; I wondered what diabetics were doing in a mental hospital? Every thirty paces a handle stuck out. These were to pull over a metal partition in the event of a fire. Suddenly he whipped a huge key from the depth of his jacket pocket and opened a door into 'Pandora's box'.

The top half of the wall and the ceiling were a smoky cream, the bottom half was a light green. The pine boarding on the floor glistened in defiance at its dull surroundings. At the far end, the tiled fireplace looked out of place, as did the eight-inch long, inch thick, strap of rubber, which sat on the mantelpiece?

Fifty patients sat at a dozen tables eating their breakfast. The clatter of metal hitting porcelain plates was deafening. Nurses ran back and forth, serving meals from the aluminium trolley. "Do you want roast beef, mince or salad for dinner to-day"? The nursing assistant was reciting this to each and every patient. I was escorted to the office door marked 'Charge Nurse', and as the door closed behind me, the silence stabbed my throbbing consciousness.

His grey-blue eyes swept over me from hair to toe. I imagined that he now knew my blood type. "Take a chair". He said, smiling, as if he meant it. "You'll be assigned to staff nurse, Capric Wally, do as he tells you and you won't go far wrong". He stood up and glided to the door. "Well! Let's go".

The white coat was draped over his body like a shroud, a capstan full strength dangled precariously between his lips. "Call me 'Cappy'" was delivered in machine-gun fashion. His eyes darted everywhere, quick and intelligent. I was introduced to the other staff rapidly, with the odd wisecrack thrown in. "Nursing assistant Ama Tird, always left with the double blank at the dominoes. Deputy charge 'Hardie Core', enrolled nurse 'Jim Duken' if he sits for more than a minute we check his pulse to see if he is still alive. This reprobate doubles as a staff nurse, 'Al Dune'".

A few of the patients introduced themselves. 'Tobac', held out a nicotine-scarred hand, the fingers were charcoal from all the burnt tissue. In his other hand, a rolled up piece of newspaper with tobacco, which was his favourite smoke? "Are you going to work here, darling? Do you smoke? Can I have a cigarette? Cappy, gave him a cigarette, which he immediately broke open, placed the tobacco in a thin line on a piece of newspaper which he folded over, licked the edge, rolled it together, then with a big toothless grin, "Have you got a light, darling?" In complete contrast a shy, handsome young lad, welcomed me to the ward. "I hope you enjoy working with us". Even a white smile, that seemed genuine. "Perhaps we will get better acquainted. It helps if you can play dominoes or crib!" I replied that I looked forward to a game. "My name is 'BB', short for 'Babe Bait', which everyone likes to call me". A sneering red headed boy with a motley complexion butted in. "You'll need to watch your back in this ward, all the patients will stick a knife up your arse as soon as look at you! His high-pitched laughter jangled my nerves as he slapped his knees in glee. "My names 'Lenske' and I'm the nicest patient in the whole hospital. I take fits, but the staff keep me safe". Walking on rapidly, I almost fell over 'Sabloki', who was bending low, to get a light for his cigarette. The patient giving him a light was moving his lighter down to the floor, 'Sabloki' followed! "I'm sorry, mate. Are you alright?" I held his muscular arm, to stop us both falling over. "Ergh!" He barked, through a row of rotten teeth and continued to try to light his cigarette. A neatly dressed gentleman, was struggling into a huge, navy blue, duthel jacket, that came down to the top of his wellie boots. "I'm Alec, it's time for me to go to work in the gardens. I'll maybe catch you later".

Then we ran down the short corridor to the dormitory. It was packed tight, with thirty plus, steel framed beds. "All patients in bed by seven o-clock". A sprint through the bathroom, which had three baths, two showers, ten toilet cubicles, a ten foot long urinal and ten wash-hand basins. Across the corridor, the spacious kitchen glistened. A squat, bald headed man, with a smile that split his face in half. "This is 'Henry Peck', patient cum head porter, the hardest worker in the hospital". His shovel-like hands crushed mine in a too friendly manner. "Very pleased to be meeting you I'm sure".

As we returned to the dining room, the patients were clearing away the table and chairs into the corner of the room, which would now revert back into the sitting room. It seemed to happen in slow motion as I watched in disbelief. His long face came to a point at the top of his hairless head. Big sad black eyes, hooked nose and small tight mouth, all projected forward from a scrawny neck, and the emaciated banana body, from which his drab clothes hung. The patient, they called him 'Stowaway', had lifted one of the easy chairs and swung it down on the deputy charges' back. "I need a B". He declared, in a pathetic monotone. This turned out to be a tranquilizer that 'Stowaway' was addicted to and the staff were attempting to wean him off. 'Hardie' had somehow managed to cushion most of the blow, but he would have a sore back for a long time. This was to be my first experience of violence, which would be so common in the future, that it became my regular nightmare.

The male and female sides were strictly segregated. Male nurses were never tolerated on the female side unless they were required to escort or restrain a violent female! It would not be uncommon for males to return from the female side with black eyes and swollen testicles! It was much more awkward to restrain females, due to their anatomy and the fact that they would scream loudly and declare they were, being raped! It was also more difficult to remain detached, when you had to hold down a beautiful girl, pull down her underwear and give her an injection in her bottom! Sometimes they would be completely naked, running round the ward screaming. Trying to wrap a blanket round them was like attempting to hold onto an eel! Some females would create a scene so that they could enjoy groping a male nurse, though some preferred a female!

Egocentric

The financial company needed to get rid of a thorn in their side. 'Ethanual' was a Hypochondriac, who had been off work for over a year, but refused to accept any lay-off plan. My assignment, if I wanted it, was to help him accept the inevitable; either return to work, or accept that he must leave without a pension, which he was not entitled to anyway! The previous therapist, Dr. Quarny, was eager to supply me with all the history of his physical and mental manifestations. "Please phone me at any time, I will be interested to know the outcome".

Sporadic episodes of paralysis, which were at odds with normal neurological pathways, bouts of acute depression, sickness, diarrhoea, headache, backache, etc, etc, etc.... I arranged an appointment for Monday, if he lived that long!

He was a handsome forty year old man, well dressed and, outwardly, healthy looking individual? "Thank you for seeing me. I feel confident that you can help me clear up this misunderstanding. The company want me to accept their conditions and simply leave, but I can't afford to do that, I need the pension plan that they offer everyone else. I have spoken to one of their ex-managers, down in Glasgow, who retired sick and got a good pension. He advised me to hang on, and they would have to give me the same".

There was no evidence of any psychosis. He seemed in touch with reality, articulate and well turned out. His belief that he was due a pension, stemmed from his need to be financially secure. In the past his illnesses had probably served him 'well', excuse the pun. I knew that if I approached the problem directly, he would quickly adopt his old defence mechanisms, and I would gain nothing. We spoke about his earlier working life. How proud his wife and daughter must have been for him. We talked about his working relations with his colleagues, holidays and adventures. He agreed to participate in relaxation, during which suggestions of success and future pride were introduced, along with self-esteem and confidence. This was reinforced by positive future orientation. His next session was set for a week later.

He phoned the day before his appointment. "I have a meeting with the company tomorrow. I want to thank you for your help. Everything seems clearer now, I feel so positive and alive. You really are amazing. If only I had seen you sooner, I would not have had to suffer that sanctimonious doctor. I cannot thank you enough. Goodbye!"

Was I the greatest, or was I the Greatest! One session and I had achieved the, seemingly, impossible. I must be the best!

It was two weeks later and I had heard nothing. I finally gave in and phoned doctor Quarny, to inform him of my amazing success and to discover the outcome of the company meeting.

"Yes, Ethanuel attended the meeting, told the board that he was a very sick man and asked when he would be receiving his pension rights! They, in response, informed him that he would be 'paid off' in four weeks time, due to his inability to work and he did not qualify for a pension".

My mouth dropped and rage pulled at my shoulder. "But, he seemed so positive when he phoned me. I thought he was prepared to return to work. He said he was delighted with everything I had done for him" Doctor Quarny gave a deep sigh. "Ethanuel has, many times, told me the same thing. Full of insight and praise for my wonderful help, but nothing changes and he continues to demand a pension that he is not entitled to. You just cannot win with these clients!"

My head had shrunk to the size of a pea, though it was still bigger than the excuse for a brain that occupied it.

Hypocondriacal clients usually believe that because they have a cough, headache or palpitations, they must be suffering from lung cancer, a tumour of the brain or heart disease! Despite reassurance from several doctors, they will continue to cling, doggedly to their belief. These people are typically anxious, sensitive individuals, who love nothing better than to discuss their symptoms, as a rationale for their belief, that they have a deadly disease!

The only thing that kept me sane, took my mind of all my concerns and made me feel almost normal was my judo training! Once a week, on a Thursday, I would trot along to the dojo, don my canvas suit and work out on a warm-up routine, randori, or sparring practice, throw and be thrown, practice hold-down's and new techniques, finally, have a session on the weights! It was all great fun, although, I was only a mediocre player, due mainly to the fact that I lacked the aggression and the fitness!

Brain Drain

It was supposed to be my day off; but the charge nurse had begged me to cover the ward, as a nurse had phoned in sick? What a bugger, but I owed him a favour for all the overtime he had put my way. I phoned the boys, to tell them I would not be going fishing with them and donned my white coat.

Fishing is probably my main interest. I dream of the 'big one' as I prepare the rod, reel, line and the lures, shiny and colourful. We would drive to the bottom of the hill then carry our gear over the heather for almost an hour, the silhouette of the stags as they cast a wary eye on the strangers. Finally, the first light of the day would highlight the loch and shout a shimmering welcome. Shoals of fish were imagined to cause all the mysterious undercurrents that danced on the waters surface.

Outwardly calm, though bubbling with anticipation, we assembled our split cane rods, threaded the five pound breaking strain, nylon line through the eyes and a multi-looped bowline would secure the all important lure. The first cast is always magical, dropping the lure at the precise point where the mountain stream pours into the loch. The wobble of the lure, as you retrieve the line, ready to flick the end of the rod when the bite occurs, now, the real fun begins. Play the fish to avoid it jumping the hook or breaking the line. Reel her in steady, if she makes a run for it let her go, keeping a slight pressure on the line, avoid a yank or you may lose the prize.

The exhausted trout is whipped onto the bank amid clapping and cheers.

They had admitted 'Soldier Donald' last night. His mother was fussing over him like a hen with only one egg. His baldhead hung low, as he walked back and forth with his mother holding his arm, looking up at his tall, gangly frame, muttering comforting words to him. When his mother left, he sat by the wall, his head in his hands. Some of the patients called him a 'mummies boy' and threw kisses at him. Lenske, came over and sat beside him. He patted his huge shoulders with one hand while sticking his fingers down his throat, as if to make himself sick. "You'll be alright here. Just take the tablets and the electric shock treatment and you'll be out in ten years time. Don't worry, I'll look after you". The other patients laughed and made clucking noises like demented hens. "If you like, I'll service your mother for you and show her how a real man can give pleasure". Donald straightened up and glowered down at Lenkse. A deadly silence shot through the ward. Huge hands pinned Lenske against the wall. I put my hand out to restrain Donald. The blissful feeling of weightlessness, as I spun through the air and landed softly on the floor? Lenske gasped as the huge fist sank deep into his stomach. Donald sat down again, his head in his hands. "Are you ok now?" I asked Donald, ignoring the squirming heap on the floor. "I hope I didn't hurt you. Sorry about that". He looked up at me with wet, blue/grey eyes from a sea of white, sagging skin. "This is terrible! My brain just will not work and all the time I'm confused and frightened. What's to become of me? Who will look after my old mother?" I said nothing, for there was no answer!

It was Sunday; so as many patients as possible were herded down to the service, at the lovely hospital church. As many as sixty to seventy patients and staff, sometimes even the matron, made up the congregation. The minister would scream, hellfire and damnation, whilst glaring down at the sinners. The organ player, who could hardly see and suffered arthritis, painfully struck up the music and an erratic response was heard from those singers who had no idea of the tune. At the mere mention of God or Jesus, a patient would leap up from the pew. "Yes, my child, I will save you!" Sometimes,

it could be ignored, but, if the patient then tried to climb into the pulpit, he or she would be taken back to the ward.

'Solo Cell' looked out at the world, as a baby looks up to it's mother. The motorbike accident had flattened his brain to a pulp; at least the wall he had decimated could be rebuilt! Every so often, he would jump up and roar, surrounding patients would either duck and cover their heads or lash out at him with fright. However, he was harmless and would just sit down again, looking about in sheer amazement.

The insurance company was dragging its heels on the payout. Though it looked a dead cert that Solo Cell would never recover, the insurers were holding out in case of a miracle! His lovely, petite wife visited every second day, her long blonde hair, shiny brown nylon, covering her shapely legs were a magnet for all eyes. She would stay a couple of hours, tantalizing the patients and staff, who would flock round her. Though obviously embarrassed by the fact that her husband ignored her and indeed seemed oblivious to her presence, she was always pleasant, asking questions about his health whilst looking up at you demurely through her eyelashes. He greedily ate the titbits she feed him then she would light a cigarette for him, which he would puff in and out but did not seem to enjoy. Before the accident, he was a chain smoker! She appeared to be the ideal nursemaid and wife.

It was over a year and Solo Cell remained in his vegetative state so the insurers had no option but to pay out what was rumoured to be a tidy sum of money. His wife never returned and although we all missed her, Solo Cell did not seem to notice that his pretty, petite wife had disappeared.

My job at the hospital was enjoyable. Seeing the way all the staff carried out their work, fitting in with each other making the ward run so smoothly. The routine also included regular tea breaks and, of course, Dominoes. Four to six staff would sit round the table, in the sitting room. A patient would sit in, merely as a spectator, and then if a nursing officer came in we would say we were playing with a patient! Honest! It seemed that the double blank was glued to Ama Tird's hand, as he always produced it, to gain a low score, which was the object of the game.

'Babe Bait' was a schizophrenic patient who was so named because females could not resist him. He was eighteen years old, long blond hair, brown eyes, chiselled features and a great personality. We both hit it of, talked about everything under the sun and we had mutual respect for each other. His admissions followed the usual path, initially a year between acute episodes, it gradually became more frequent until he required constant supervision. The tablets helped to dampen the hallucinations, but when he went home he would stop taking them and become psychotic again! "I don't want to be on tablets for the rest of my life. Each time I stop taking them, I feel great for a while, but then it all returns; suspiciousness, anxiety, anger, fears and so many voices and sounds. When will I escape this torment?"

Our first job in the morning was a cup of tea with the night nurse, who would report all that happened during the night. The written report in the notebook, would usually read, 'All patients slept well', but the verbal report was much more detailed. "Tobac, was round the lockers, stealing tobacco. Lenkse, had a wee fit". This was the norm for these two. "Ginger has been kept away from the taps. He is down for his twice weekly, straight, electro-convulsive therapy, so no water and no breakfast!" Then, any rumours discussed, bits added on, until it assumed the accolade of a full-blown scandal. It is said, that a seed of truth, can sprout a legend! Well, hospitals can be the greenhouse for these seeds!

We were then divided into two groups. One group would get the patients up, washed and dressed, the other, would work through the bathing list. Then it was time for the patients breakfast. A couple of patients would set out the tables and chairs that were stacked in the corner of the sitting cum dinning room. When the meal was over, the plates, knives, forks and cups were put through to the kitchen for Pector to wash. The table and chairs were stacked back into the corner. It was time for the 'cures'!

Cappy, being the senior staff nurse, wheeled the medicine trolley out and placed the kardex, which contained all the patients prescribed medicines and recording sheets on the side. He would have all the medications already set out on the trolley and all the recording sheets signed! Two patients would sit at a side table, one with glasses of orange juice, the other with a bowl of hot water and a dishcloth. All the patients would line up in single file, take their tablets or syrup, then a drink of orange juice and put their glass into the bowl of hot water, which was rinsed out and then dried by the allocated patient.

The deputy superintendent was a consultant psychiatrist, who was responsible for our ward. A rotund, fresh complexioned, balding gentleman. Always very clean and dapper, he was extremely meticulous in everything that he did. In many ways, I was reminded of Agathas' 'Piorot'! All the patients and staff respected him, for he was kind, considerate and sincere. If the occasion demanded, he could be very stern and severe! As he did his round of the patients, they would stand up and shake his hand. Patients on the garden squad would then go to the back door to don their duthel jackets and welly boots.

A week in my new room at the nurse's home and I was surprised to hear a knock on the door! Mr. Quint, a charge nurse of a long-term ward at the hospital, was filling the doorway. "Just thought I would welcome you to the hospital, see that you are settling in ok." His mass of flab almost filled the room as he accepted my invitation to enter. "That's a lovely radio; may I hear its tone?" He reached over me to switch it on, his body lingering too long, as his corpulence pressed against me. "Music is so important." His hard 'fish like' eyes ogled the guitar in the corner that could only manage three chords, before it detuned itself. "Do you caress the frets?" Again his body rubbed over me, more intimately this time and his hand brushed my inside leg. I suddenly realized that he was coming on to me and in my stupidity had misinterpreted his intentions. My slow-witted reactions had obviously made him think he was onto a 'nice boy'! "You'll need to go, please, I have to be on shift in an hour." My request only served to inflame his ardour. "Perhaps you would like me to help you change. It's important to look smart." His fat fingers started to unbutton my trousers, with remarkable rapidity. Pushing, with the strength that shock can give you, he oozed out the door, which was slammed and the key turned. At last, I could breathe, as the fear and revulsion subsided.

It would have been easy to sail blissfully on forever, but I had not left the well-paid driving job, only to be a nursing assistant. I had to be a real nurse, get a qualification. Perhaps that would stop me from being dumped on the scrap heap again! During my dinner hour, I strode, determinedly, down to the classroom, which adjoined the nurses' home, where I stayed. Knocking on the door marked Principle Tutor, a distant voice responded. "One moment, I'll be right with you".

Dark bushy eyebrows and the sharp, piercing eyes, it was Mr. Mortiman! "Hello there, what can I do for you?" The voice, disconcertingly soft and melodious. "I would like to take up nurse training. Can you tell me how to go about it?"

"You're lucky! Next month there is an intake of first year students. Unfortunately, because you do not have the required qualifications it will be necessary to sit the entrance examination. Be here next Monday at ten and you can sit the test".

Thanking him, I walked away despondently. The fact that I was as thick as 'two short planks' and 'dimmer than a candle in a hurricane' meant that I was destined to remain a lowly assistant. Back at the ward my problem was shared with the staff nurse Aintie Smirt. "Is no problemo my good man, I will teach you all you need to know, just leave it all to me".

True to his word, every time we had a spare moment, he would bombard me with questions and help me work out the answers. "There are ten chickens in a cage, which is made up of iron bars and covered by strong mesh. A fox digs a tunnel, under the wire and into the cage. He kills one of the chickens and eats it, greedily. How many chickens are left?" You may think, the obvious answer is nine, but the correct answer is, none; they all escape through the tunnel that the fox came in by! This was a good example, of following what is expected, because, in actual fact, wouldn't the

chickens be too terrified to move, far less run into a tunnel! My brain was buzzing, threatening to short-circuit. At night in my tiny room, at the nurse's home, I would attempt to swat up on all aspects of nursing literature. To my left, with his ghetto blaster, that had only one volume setting, loud, resided Lurch, so named because he was covered in plucks, walked so awkwardly and spoke in a slow, baleful drawl. The thudding bass section of 'Procal Harem' thundered in. To my right, Aintie Smirt, was noisily investigating the delights of 'Blousy', the delectable, blonde student nurse.

It was time to sit the entrance exam! I was on my own in the classroom. Questions, about the number of bricks in a pyramid? What number follows the last four? Which triangles fit into the square? I got three questions right, name, address and date of birth. Somehow I passed? They must have needed to make up the numbers.

Macho Man

His name was Clair Bair, could I help him deal with his panic attacks? He was a train driver. "Out of the blue, for no reason, I start to sweat buckets, my heart pounds and I know I will die if I don't get off the train".

Married, with two grown-up sons, enjoyed gardening and going for long walks with his wife. Nothing significant in his childhood, no financial worries, marriage was good, no upheavals, in fact the only apparent factor would seem to be his middle age! Possible existential crisis! Despite his thin body, grey hair and watery blue eyes, he tried, very hard, to give the impression, "Get on the wrong side of me and you're history".

It was decided that I would teach him relaxation, during which I would get him to experience increasingly higher levels of panic situations, whilst remaining relaxed. This should work, according to the principles of 'reciprocal inhibition', which states, 'You cannot experience opposite emotions at the same time', i.e. Tension/ relaxation, Happiness/sadness, etc. Despite the session going well, when it came to driving, he still suffered panic attacks. So, we moved on to try, 'Flooding'! By increasing the panic, to bursting point, we should, in theory, blow out the emotional content of the situation. It didn't. Cognitive therapy seemed a reasonable approach. What he said to himself before he panicked, the behavioural cycle, antecedent-behaviour-consequences. Break the chain and you break the outcome. We didn't get of the ground with that one! Positive future-orientation, was our next great hope. "Imagine you have had a successful train journey. Feel how that feels, see yourself looking very pleased with yourself, hear all the passengers thanking you for doing so well". It worked, but only for three days. He again started to panic!

Clair was starting to sense my exasperation. "Please don't give up on me, keep trying as long as it takes". His watery-blue eyes searched mine for a glimmer of hope.

"We know what doesn't work, so we just need to find out what does". I said, mainly because that was what he needed to hear.

In my dreams, trains were jumping off the track and exploding. Something didn't make sense! What was I missing? These techniques probably failed because I had neglected to assess the underlying problem in enough depth, and certainly without pinpointing the actual motivating factors behind the phobia. Although he was unable to identify any reason for his problem, that did not necessarily mean there was not an occurrence in his past that he had somehow forgotten or had refused to acknowledge!

Overtime Marriage

My girlfriend accepted my proposal; we got married nine months later. A further nine months and we were chuffed and overwhelmed to have a beautiful baby girl! I worked my spare time as a waiter at the station hotel. If I were on the back shift at the hospital then I would work breakfasts at the hotel, dinners, in the evening when I was doing my week of early shifts at the hospital. During the summer months, the hotel would take on foreign students and sometimes it was necessary to split them up, otherwise they would probably knife each other. Their highly excitable nature meant that, at times, it could get quite hairy! Mr. Tophe did a great job as the headwaiter. He was efficient and organized all the staff into a smooth working team. After meals, he would set up a blackboard in the empty dinning room and give the foreign students English lessons. One of these students had no need of lessons; he was a linguist, speaking fluently in eight languages! He was very ambitious and went on to open his own restaurant.

As usual, I didn't believe that I was earning enough money, so, when the chance came up to work as a security guard and driver, it seemed too good an opportunity to pass by. At weekends and days off, it was into the driving seat, going round the town picking up the takings and data sheets of businesses and taking them to Aberdeen. There we were met by another van, which took the stuff to Glasgow. At the weekend, the run was at night, getting back home at midnight! This was great fun, until a delay on the night run caused me to miss the connecting van for Glasgow! It was eleven o-clock and the control centre informed me that I would have to carry on to Glasgow, which was a further three hundred mile round trip! This would normally be ok, but my shift at the hospital started in seven hours time, which meant only two hours sleep! Thankfully, the ward I worked in was settled and I somehow managed to ease my weary bones through the shift.

Three years later, my adorable son was born! Still my insecurity clawed at my guts. The need to earn extra cash was not being satisfied. The headwaiter, at the hotel, moved to a bar restaurant and asked me if I would like a job as a wine waiter there. "There are good tips to be made and better crack with the punters!" "I'm your man". I said, wondering how I could squeeze more than twenty-four hours out of a day.

Somehow, I coped! One night, after working at the bar, it was near midnight and I was enjoying my walk home, as it was quiet and still. Rounding a corner, I heard him before I had the misfortune to see him! Swearing and cursing everyone and everything under the moon, he was struggling to walk a straight line, obliviously banging into walls and lampposts. On the other side of the street, carrying their haversacks and helmets, a group of brickies, who had obviously just left the building site, were laughing among themselves. Suddenly they ran across the street, knocking the drunken man down, they began to kick and rain blows down on him as they swung their haversacks! He was too far gone to defend himself from the crushing blows. It was all too much for my delicate sense of justice! Before I could even think it through, I had jumped into the middle of the frenzied pack! "That's enough, lads. You'll kill the man if you don't stop!" It all happened so quickly and bizarrely that the group froze and a ghastly hush contaminated the proceedings. At any moment, I expected them to turn their attack on me! I figured, if I could flatten the first two that moved, then maybe the others would move on? Logic informed me that it was probably going to be a crucifixion! As if by magic, they all walked off together, laughing and chatting about their day, as if nothing had happened! Turning to the drunk, who by this time had climbed upright, I asked if he was alright. Barging past me, he continued on his way, cursing and swearing he weaved his crazy steps home.

Next morning it was back to my normal Job, at the hospital. The first person to greet my bleary gaze was the mouthy drunk! He had apparently presented himself at his ward, for recovering alcoholics. When they noticed all his cuts and bruises, they transferred him to the hospital ward. He was suffering from a devastating hangover and although there were no broken bones, every movement resulted in excruciating pain. As he had no memory whatsoever of his 'night out', I informed the charge nurse of my heroic actions, concerning last nights events. "You're a bloody idiot!" He shouted at me. "You should be in the bed next to him!" I had obviously made a slight error of judgment!

My bar job was good fun and I made plenty of tips. You had to be polite and chatty, yet quick and efficient. One evening I was told the price of some of the wines had gone up, but the prices on the menus had not yet been altered. A few punters queried the anomaly and were informed that new menus, with the price rise, had still to be printed! When the police began making enquires, I decided to make a quick exit! The establishment changed proprietors soon after.

My first week of nightshift at the hospital passed without incident. The dormitory was quiet; all the patients seemed to know that I needed the rest! My other jobs seemed to be fitting in smoothly, but I was getting less and less sleep! 'What had I done today?' 'Had everything been completed?' 'Was there anything that I had forgotten?' Tomorrow was my night off, so I could drive the van to Aberdeen. 'Please don't let me miss the other, connecting van; I'm on breakfast at the hotel in the morning'. 'But what am I thinking of? My night shift is in a couple of hours. Isn't it?' My mind froze over! It was like looking through frosted glass! Suddenly, nothing made any sense. My mind and body were shutting down and I could do nothing to prevent a total collapse!

The phone must have rung, because my wife came up to the bedroom. "It's the hospital! They say you were supposed to be on duty tonight and they are asking when you are coming in". I went downstairs, to the phone. "I am taking the night off. Just cannot be bothered going to work. Goodnight!" Returning to my bed, I slept for two days!

On returning to work, the night superintendent called me to his office. "Sorry about taking nights off" He seemed to be listening with exaggerated attentiveness, was I going to be sent home? "Afraid I just overdid my part-time work. From now on, my work at the hospital takes first place. I have already packed in most of my other jobs". There was a long delay and horrible thoughts passed through my mind. "Off you go to your ward. We will put this down to overwork and say no more about it". I had survived a possible sacking. Urgent measures were required, to avoid any more disasters in my life. By being stricter on my time and only accepting work when it fitted in with my work and rest, finally I got quality time at home. It was great to be able to spend time with my children and be more involved in their lives. How strange to realize that they were changing from day to day. All too soon, they would be adults and I would lose them forever!

Student Daze

All the first year students were presented with a booklet containing the syllabus for our, three year, psychiatric training. The booklet was a record of our practical instruction and experience. Any ward we worked in, we had to get it signed by the charge nurse or ward sister and the clinical instructor. It comprised of an Introductory Period, which included, Ward management, Bed-making, General care of patients, Serving and feeding of patients and Nursing procedures. Then, it was onto the Advanced Nursing. This included, Psychiatric nursing, Nursing of patients presenting special problems, such as, adolescent, elderly, suicidal, epileptic, patients with depraved and degraded habits, patients who refuse food, etc, etc. Practical nursing was next, with Physical examination, rectal examination, vaginal examination (Female nurses only). Lumber puncture, Marrow puncture, etc, etc. Finally it was necessary to have instruction and experience in Reception, Geriatric, Long term, Occupational therapy and physically ill wards and departments.

The first years training was fascinating and fun. Most of the time we spent in the classroom studying biology, physiology, psychology, anthropology and anyotherology! There was the occasional trip, up to the hospital wards, but only to the pristine admission wards or the tidy, small, short-term wards. I discovered that the 'Insulin' ward, had originally been used for patients with severe chronic problems. A sufficient dose of insulin was administed, to maintain the patient in a state of coma. They would only be roused for feeding, and then returned to sleep! The nursing was very intensive and costly; the results were not encouraging. It was presently being used as a store!

The classes were interesting and mostly concentrated on preparation for the three years of study that lay ahead. "Par, stands for, Practice Active Recall, Which I want you always to remember". Mr. Mortiman would emphasize with his wonderful modulated voice. Gradually he would increase the content of his lectures as we were guided toward more intensive and difficult material. His favourite lecture seemed to be, the examination of urine! We would each be given a clear beaker and told to provide a sample of urine; this was then studied for colour, smell, sediment, cloudiness and finally he would dip his index finger and put it in his mouth. "It usually has a slightly acidic taste!" Unknown to us, he would change the finger he put in his mouth! "But it is easier and more hygienic, to use a litmus paper. Acid will turn the blue paper red." Some of the students had their fingers half way to their mouths and breathed a sigh of relief, when they realized it was a joke. Anyway, it had an alkaline taste and was not at all pleasant!

Then we were introduced to the 'Clinical Instructor', Mr. A Tinker. He would teach us the practical skills of nursing. These included; bed making, storage of linen, mattresses, rubber liners, pillows etc, bathing, physical examination, enemas, setting out procedural trays, i.e. neurological examination, blood specimens, etc, all of which I detested! Rather disconcertingly, Mr. A Tinker would say, 'you know!' in either the middle or the end of a sentence, sometimes both! It was difficult to keep a straight face when he spoke. "The turndown of the top sheet, over the cellular blanket, you know, should measure from the elbow to the fingertips, you know!" Flucker would intercede. "But some of us, you know, have shorter forearms than others, you know, sir!" He was obviously aware of the off-takers and would look at you in a condescending manner. "And some people, you know, have smaller brains, you know!" He was very precise in everything that he taught and would spend hours making sure everyone understood and could carry out the procedures.

When it came to dispensing medicines, in a ward setting, most of the staff nurses were decidedly nervous. This was usually because, most had long since dispensed with 'proper working practices', preferring instead to make the job quicker and easier. Ideally, two nurses should dispense the medication, one reading the prescription, from the kardex, the other, putting out the medication to the patient. In real life, this was not practical, because you had to get all the work done rapidly, so that we could get on with the essential daily game of dominoes or crib! Everything else took second place! Senior nurses, like Cappy, knew all the patients medicines and would simply fill in the kardex and have all the medicines sitting in a row of glasses, ready to dish out to the patients. Where 'good practice', would take thirty to forty minutes, Jo would be finished and have the dominoes on the table by ten minutes! It was therefore a pain in the butt, when Mr. A Tinker decided that the students should dispense the medicines, or help with the bathing, in a particular ward.

There were thirty-six students in the class, mostly female! Dot was a mature student, face of granite with an attitude to match. Then there was Genna, the beautiful mother figure. Her dark brown hair, big, soft brown eyes, full sexual mouth and body, turning most of the lads into drooling, phallic inadequates. The class got on well together, fluctuating from helpful encouragement to goading banter and jokes, intended to rouse the aspirations of the opposite sex. Jon the Stick, was oblivious to all this joviality, unless it suited his purpose. He was brilliant and had only condescended to join the class to get away from his parents, who kept on at him to take his place at university. "You must keep up the family tradition". Jon was too busy having a party, which he had decided, could be more easily achieved at the nurses' home, with its endless supply of female nurses. Flucker had a mean streak, which became apparent when he came under the least bit of stress. He would start cursing and miscalling everyone in the class. At these times, we would drop the L from his name, which always failed to amuse him.

At the end of the second year, we were subjected to a preliminary examination, which identified the prize students. Several students had fallen by the way. The rest were destined to reach the glorious rank of 'staff nurse'. That is, all but Lurch! Who realised his stomach was too delicate to withstand eating his hospital food, informally known as 'gash', after performing a manual evacuation of a patients bowels or being covered in muck and blood, whilst stopping a wrist slashing suicide. He joined the civil service and did very well there.

The third year was ridiculous, all the stuff we should have learned the previous two years, was compounded by, pharmacology, medical diseases, psychiatry and behavioural psychology. I enjoyed studying, but how could I remember enough to pass the final examination? By using words, like, 'How Right U Feel Puffing That Fag', I was reminded of the bones in the arm and leg. Humerus, Radius, Ulna, Femur, Patella, Tibia and Fibula. Sometimes I would read an article and have no idea what it meant. After a cup of tea, I would read it again and it would all make sense! The best time for me to study was immediately after a class. I could go over the lesson, at my own speed and this helped to nail it into my brain. The final examination would be in two parts, written and oral. My only hope was to memorise the questions that were being asked most frequently and ignore the rest!

The previous month, we had to submit a case history of one of the patients we had worked with. I choose to write about 'Tiptoe', so called because he walked everywhere on his toes! He was seventeen years of age, red hair, sandpaper skin, six feet tall, dumb and seemed unable to understand anything. Whenever he was allowed into the toilet, he would head straight for the tap, stick his head under it and pour the water down his throat. The result was that he went high as a kite, racing up and down the ward knocking people and chairs to the floor. Tiptoe, had been a normal child, up to the age of five, when he was given a routine vaccination for measles! His relatives were informed that the chances of a reaction, in this severe form, were one hundred thousand to one. Tragically, he was the one.

"Now turn over the paper in front of you and start to write. You have two and a half hours". The questions seemed to be in a foreign language. Disjointed words sprang from the page. Explain?

Rationalise? Consider??? I closed my eyes and told my brain that it knew the answers and if it did not we would hazard a guess.

Missing Memories

It was Clair's fifth session and he agreed to the use of a regression technique. We started with the ideo-motor response. This uses the involuntary lifting of a finger to indicate at what age a problem period is evident. By asking questions, relating to this time, we should reveal what lies there. "I went to bed first, being the youngest, later my brother would come to bed. Sis slept in her own room". He looked agitated, eyes swung rapidly from side to side under heavy eyelids. His mouth moved but no sound emerged.

"In a few moments you will awaken feeling refreshed and relaxed. If the time is right you will then be able to accept the reason for your problem, you may not need to bring the material into consciousness".

On opening his eyes, Clair, spoke of the utter confusion he had felt. "All kinds of feelings bombarded my mind. I used to get these feelings when I was young; I would go to the dance at the 'Lido', pick on the biggest, meanest looking son of a bitch and try to punch his lights out. This happened every week, I was so angry and mixed up".

When making his next appointment, I suggested that he might like to report any dreams that may occur over this time.

Qualified

As luck would have it, some of the questions in the final exam were in line with what I had memorised. It was a relief to see a question on the subject of 'curator bonis' as it was a topical subject at this time. This is regarding responsibility for patients who are deemed unfit due to their mental state. Then came the question, about identifying symptoms of Simple Schizophrenia, with a treatment regime. Some answers only required a one-word answer, while others were a minimum of thirty words. The next day we attended for the oral part of the exam. I was quizzed, regarding the case history about 'Tiptoe', the instruments used in various procedures, caring for bedsores, the different admission protocols and the latest scandal round the hospitals!

It took a month before we got the results. Yes! I was a qualified staff nurse. At last I felt, maybe this would give me some job security. I proudly flaunted the blue strip on the shoulder of my white coat!

As junior staff nurses, we were chaperoned round our allocated ward, in our stiff, white coats. The honeymoon was over all too soon and our names were on the ward timesheet, along with one charge nurse, two deputies, and four staff, three enrolled and four assistant nurses. I had been allocated back to my first ward, Pandora's box! It was time for the harsh reality of 'patient care'.

Religiously, I followed 'Cappy', the senior staff nurse; hoping no one would realize my fear of incompetence! Thankfully, the strict routine made it easy to pick up and I soon felt I was part of the team.

Some of the others were not so lucky! Dot, had ended up in a psycho-geriatric ward. Her duties included safeguarding a particularly disturbed lady called 'Cynthia', who had a propensity for eating everything she saw! Whilst feeding a bed-ridden patient, Dot looked up to see 'Cynthia' eating potatoes, out of the food trolley, which was roasting hot! Lunging at her, she slapped her hard across the face. Cynthia crashed to the floor laughing, and stuffing the remaining handful of potato into her scorched mouth. Dot's face dropped, as she spotted the ward sister staring in horror. She was immediately hauled along to the matrons' office, never to be seen again, well, not as a nurse anyway!

A frightening racket emanated from the kitchen, as dinner plates were shattered on the tiled floor. Metal containers screeched as they shot across the top of the aluminium oven. Worst of all was the sickening crunch, of bone, against the concrete window ledge. Henry Peck, the kitchen porter, had suffered a major epileptic seizure! Thrashing about on the kitchen floor, the blood poured from his head, drawing a crazy pattern on the white tiles.

The rubber pad, that had pride of place on the mantle piece over the fire, was rammed into his mouth, so that he would not bit his tongue or choke himself. He was then turned onto his, left lateral side. His face was red and bloated and he began to whisper in a slur, which gradually became louder and clearer. He was yelling all the swear words he knew over and over again. Stitches were poked into the huge slit on his cranium and a dressing was plastered on top, looking, for all the world, like a turban.

The next day, Henry was back in the kitchen, washing pans, stacking plates and, optimistically, making his plans on how to spend the money he hoped to win from the Saturday football draw. "Me and Effie, will get married, buy a Mini Austin and we will go for a long run in the country".

Yet again, the two brothers returned home to find their mother cowering in a corner, trembling and bleeding. Their, black sheep, brother 'Asbro' had, for the umpteenth time, beaten her up and thrashed the house. A combination of 'mothers tongue' epilepsy, psychopathy and a gallon of 'giraffe' wine had again tipped him over the edge.

As he was only out of the hospital on pass, it was simply a case of phoning us up, dragging him up to the ward and chucking him in the door. It was suppertime and the tables were being set as he paced up and down between the tables, looking, no doubt, for a way out and gathering his anger at the injustice of it all. Breathing heavily as puny muscles twitched, his unruly black hair was carelessly flicked from his flaccid face. Jim and I were assigned to watch him until the duty doctor arrived to decide his fate. Grabbing a knife, he held it high as he lunged toward me; hate twisting his features and doubling his determination.

Crossing my arms above my head I blocked the downward strike, holding his wrist and stepping to the side, the twisting movement threw him onto the floor with a jarring thud. As he lay still, the knife was returned to the table; we lifted him up, threw him onto a chair and dared him to move. My judo training had come in useful. The duty doctor decided that he should remain in our ward until the consultant saw him in the morning. He was warned, that any more trouble and he would spend the night in the cells.

It was morning and we were preparing for the doctors round; faces washed and shaved, clothes clean and tidy and then we did the patients. Of course, Asbro got up in his usual girn, but this time it was Chuckies turn to face his wrath, as he was slated from heaven to hell. 'You are not a proper nurse. Your mother must be ashamed of you, picking on innocent, decent people like me'. Now, unfortunately, Chuckie had been out last night at a very boozy party and his 'tender loving care' was at rock bottom. So, when Asbro took a swing at his chin, he 'lost it'. Half a dozen quick, powerful punches were landed before we could restrain him. Asbro lay on the bathroom tiles crying his little heart out. 'I'm going to report you to the doctor, you pisshead bully', standing up and looking in the mirror at his bruises, he smiled 'this will cost you your job'. We held tightly onto Chuckie as his muscles tightened.

The patients all lined up as the consultant, Poirot look-alike, marched along, quizzing them as to the state of their health. On reaching the battle scarred Asbro, who eagerly shook his hand, the consultant asked, 'What on earth happened to you?' Casting a filthy look at Chuckie, he spat out his venom. 'That nurse attacked me for no reason whatsoever'. Consultant turned to look at the guilty nurse, then, as he moved on to the next patient, 'I'm sure you must have done something to deserve your chastisement'.

Alcohol was an all too common problem, with patients and staff. Even when the ward organized a weekly drinks night, there was always someone trying to get more than their fair share. After supper, on payday, when the patients received their money for working in the gardens, grounds, laundry or ward duties, for patients with no parole, the nurse would discreetly take the order and money, from patients allowed to drink! They were rationed to a maximum of four cans of beer, spirits were not allowed. The nurse would then go to the supermarket, buy all the cans and any cigarettes, there was usually a couple of pounds over to cover the petrol! On his return, the patients would congregate in the toilet area and the cans dished out. The staff strictly supervised all this, so that everyone got their fair share and the ones not drinking were kept out of the way. It even saved on medication, because they usually didn't require night sedation, or only a minimal amount! It was all a good laugh and the patients enjoyed the privilege.

But, alas, there is always a fly in the ointment! One lad, who had suffered a brain injury in an accident, would sometimes manage to smuggle in a couple of cans or a miniature of whisky! When sober, this guy was the most pleasant and helpful person on the planet. With one drink, he was transformed into a homicidal maniac! It was like a 'Hyde and Jekyll' scenario. Eyes glazed over, taut muscles and lips pursed, the head went down and he would charge, arms flailing and feet kicking. Fortunately, his coordination left a lot to be desired, so we would take him to the ground and hold him until the threshing stopped, before he was released. He would have no recollection of the incident and there was nothing to be gained from any further mention of it! One of the staff, Cappy, made the usual pig of himself. "This will keep me warm, when I go home on the bike, in all that snow!" he decided to go home early and we were given the pleasure of putting the patients to bed. A brief report to the night shift and the day shift all headed home, through the raging snowy blizzard.

Al Dune, was driving back to the ward the next morning, when he saw the wheel sticking out of the snow? His pushbike had taken our drunken staffy into the ditch and he had slept there all night! Stiff and frozen, 'Cappy the snowman' was stretchered round to the hospital ward and treated for hypothermia. A week later, he was back at work. "I need to get another pushbike, that one I have used to know the way home, but now it seems to have lost its sense of direction"!

"Would you go along to the Insulin ward for an hour, to let the nurse off for his tea break?" It was good to get a break from the ward, see something different. The Insulin ward was currently being used for recovering alcoholics and only required one staff nurse. There were only ten patients, male and female, all seemed pleasant, well dressed and were sitting in groups chatting and drinking tea. I joined one of the groups, was given a cup of tea and after introductions they continued their topic of conversation. "I'm sure I can stay off the drink this time." Her face was puffy, bags under her eyes and red blotches on her nose and cheeks. "If I just keep going to the Alcoholics Anonymous meetings and take my Antibuse tablets. It was touch and go the last time I took a drink with these tablets, I was so sick I thought I would die". Other patients spoke of similar problems, but they all seemed so positive that this time it would be different!

As I walking back from the toilet, Mr. Tot, introduced himself. He was dark haired, pale faced, very well dressed and seemed eager to talk to me. "Would you care for a cigarette"? As usual, I had run out of cigarettes so was delighted to accept. He kindly proffered his expensive lighter. Leaning forward to light the cigarette, I felt a sickening crunch as my front teeth snapped and my nose flattened, from the force of his forehead on my face! His hands were round my throat as he attempted to strangle me. Breaking the hold, I threw him onto the floor and pinned him there. He struggled furiously and I felt myself becoming weaker as I became aware of the pain and blood in my mouth, my stomach gurgled, longing to regurgitate all the tea it contained!

I heard the shout of surprise from the nurse, as he returned from his break and saw the two of us squirming on the floor. As he took over the job of holding the patient, I drew up five millimetres of Diazepam and injected it into the upper outer quadrant, of his bum. My reflection in the mirror was not a pretty sight. Maybe this was what they meant by the dangers of smoking?

Even as a staff nurse, the pay was low! This was the reason why many nurses had a part-time job and many were leaving. Even the government recognized that if recruitment of students did not pick up, the National Health Service would not have enough nurses to run their hospitals! Some wards were closing in general as well as psychiatric hospitals. The up side was that we could get as much overtime as we wanted.

The health minister at that time, Barbara Castles, commissioned the now famous 'Halsbury Report'. This recommended a massive rise in pay for all nurses, especially qualified! All the nurses were amazed, agog and watering at the mouth with anticipation. Every space, in ward papers and magazines, was crammed with calculations of the possible increase on the basic rate, night, weekend, overtime rate and the rate for different grades of staff. Surely, it was impossible that the government would pass these massive pay increases! Imagine the jubilation, when it was not only accepted, but would be backdated for several months!

Again, there wasn't a vacant space in any paper, that didn't contain a nurse's scribble of long and complicated workings out of every pound, shilling and pence we were to receive. Previously poor nurses were going on holiday's abroad, buying cars and putting deposits down on houses! There was a bonanza whirlwind of spending. At last nurses, felt appreciated and acknowledged for their hard work and dedication. We were the happiest bunnies on the planet! The euphoria would last for a couple of years, before inflation, rent rises and minimal pay increases, would see our lead being eroded and once again we were 'poor little angels'! We were back to the 'Cinderella Service'.

Driving Force

He looked like; 'Death warmed up'. His face merged with the whites of his eyes and the hands shook as they pushed back white lank hair. Clair, had finally got down to his 'driving force'.

"All week, I've been having the weirdest dreams. As I try to make sense of them, my muscles start to twitch and pictures flash rapidly, in black and white. These pictures seem to suggest something that is too horrible for my head to take in". His facial muscles tensed and relaxed spasmodically, the shoulders hunched up as he braced himself to continue. "I'm looking down from the ceiling, see myself lying in bed". Stops to breathe. "Something hugs me tightly from behind. At first, it is warm and comforting, but then it takes over my whole body. I cannot breathe, with the pain and terror; my entire body is on fire. I feel as though I might die. Waking up gasping, the bed soaked from urine and vomit. My brother slaps me across the legs. "Get fresh sheets and pillows, I'll help you change the bed". Clairs shoulders had dropped, breathing deeply he wiped the tears from his eyes. "I remember, I often suffered from diarrhoea, for a time I had black-outs, chunks of my childhood are a complete blank".

His staring eyes dared me to confirm what his conscious mind could not accept. There was no therapeutic gain in forcing him to make sense of his childhood horrors. "I'm going to help you enjoy a deep state of hypnosis, then allow your unconscious mind to resolve those experiences and accept that they are in the past. This will help to resolve your reaction and let you move on into the future. Your mind has made the wisest choice, by blanking out those memories; we have no right to change that decision. How does that feel to you?"

"I like it, I like it a lot. It seems to make sense of it all". He was beaming as he lay back and closed his eyes.

By simply asking Clair, to carry out the relaxation, he had done so often before, relaxing each limb, breathing gently into the stomach, acknowledging his heart beat and counting down from one hundred in three's. "You can now allow yourself to drift gently down into the deepest state, and now, even deeper. Such a nice safe feeling". He was now ready to begin!

"The deep part of your mind George, can allow the index finger, of the right hand, to rise up high in the air, confirming that it accepts and consolidates all that we have discussed. Will it now resolve the hurt and anguish from the past, allowing you to put it all behind you and go happily forward into a bright and optimistic future?" As I spoke, the finger raised high in the air. "As your finger descends slowly you may feel the purifying surge through your body and mind, as everything is consolidated. Such a good feeling".

It is amazing that hypnosis is so misunderstood and mistrusted. After all, it is a natural phenomenon that occurs most days of our lives. All hypnosis is 'self hypnosis'! We experience a trance state when we are driving, you got there but you cannot remember how! That feeling when you drift of to sleep, or when you first awaken. Hypnosis, has been described, as an altered state of consciousness, when access is gained to the vast subconscious. It is a powerful tool in the healing of the mind and body. The therapeutic applications are endless and much more empirical research is needed if it is ever going to be fully accepted for what it is, The Panacea!

The word comes from the Greek for sleep, hypnos. It was first used, for therapeutic purposes by Mesmer, in the eighteenth century, and he called it 'Mesmerism'. In the nineteenth century, James Braid gave it the name 'hypnosis', which was also used by Charot, under whom Sigmund Freud studied.

As teenagers, Hugh and I practiced on our friends, who for whatever reason became unavailable and we lost touch with many of them? Simple tricks, feet sticking to the floor, water tasting like wine, arm elevation, painlessly sticking pins through their flesh! On one pretty, shapely female, the suggestion that she was roasting in the sun and required to remove clothing to cool down, was most revealing, until she got down to her bra, which contained piles of tissues. Post-hypnotic suggestion was to tell a subject, under hypnosis, that they were unable to remember the number five. On waking, the subject was asked to count up to ten, each time they would miss out the number five, when asked why, they could not explain it.

The fact is all hypnosis is self-hypnosis. The hypnotist is simply guiding you into a trance state, which you decide to accept or reject. Although it is stated that you cannot be made to do anything that you would not normally do, the example of the girl stripping down to her bra, was made 'normal' by suggesting that she was hot. The extreme of this might be, telling a hypnotized subject that the man they first see when they open their eyes will be a 'serial sex attacker' and if not persuaded otherwise, will attack their child/wife/mother. Place a baseball bat in their hands, turn them to face an innocent man 'now open your eyes' -----?

The brain is capable of amazing feats of memory, healing, problem solving and generating ideas. It can also work against you, in the belief that it is defending you. Phobias are the minds way of helping you avoid problems that you had in the past. There are many, 'psychosomatic' problems, that can be traced back to a defence mechanism.

Night Duty

With a few months staffing under my belt I was roistered to go on night shift! This would be for two months and would mean extra money. Some of the patients, were escorted up to the Attic dormitory, at seven-thirty. The more disturbed patients slept in the ward dormitory. Two nurses sat in an alcove at the window, from where you could see the whole dormitory. The beds were only inches apart, so sometimes when a scuffle broke out we had to jump over the beds to break it up. During the night it was so cold we had to wrap a blanket around ourselves because the huge radiator beside us was always cold. 'It's at the end of the line' the engineers reliably informed us.

The patients were given their night sedation in the ward, and then marched up to the 'chapels' dormitory on the next floor. Clothes, would be stripped off, rolled up and chucked into the drawer, under their bed. This was, usually, a very quiet, ritualistic procedure; the only noise would be the springs singing as they snuggled under the blanket and sheet. A final head count, the 'Bed State' filled in and the nurse could then get a blanket out, place his favourite chair under the night lamp and 'rest his eyes'!

It was a terrible inconvenience, but protocol dictated that the night superintendent must do a check during the night! At midnight, they would begin at the hospital admission ward, then work their way round. As they left to go to the next dormitory, the nurse, from the previous ward, would phone to warn them and they would stand at the dormitory door to greet them. "All present and correct, nurse Macgonacle?" "Yes sir." Settling back into his warm chair and wrapping the blanket around him, he slept for about six hours!

"Morning sleepy head." It was the junior, round the house. His job was to let staff off for meals and take tea round in the morning. Macgonacle gave an incoherent grunt as he tried to taste the tea. His mind somehow coped with the fact that, in a couple of hour's time, he would be stacking baking trays and loading delivery vans at the bakery, which was his second job!

I could not move! The ropes, wound tightly round my body, seemed to hold me in a paralysed state. The patients had descended on Lensky, an epileptic who constantly bullied the more vulnerable, making them pander to his vile sexual delights. Some poked his eyes; others kicked him between his scrawny legs while some had thrown a rope over an exposed rafter. Body jerking in its last grand-mal seizure, nose pumping jets of scarlet blood, as the noose cut deep into his neck. My struggle intensified the depth of my paralyses as the terror engulfed me. "Get up" they howled in a raging torrent "Get up". Peering under the fortified shuttering, that was my eyelid; I was blinded by the floodlight before me.

"What do you think you are doing, sleeping on duty?" Night superintendent, Miss Franken, the hospital version of, 'Witch finder General'. "Go and wash your face in cold water. Report to my office immediately after your shift!" Scanning the serene sea of beds, with cruel pinprick eyes, she floated out the door, which opened and closed imperceptibly.

As I washed my face, I cursed my affliction. The car-crash happened eight years ago. It was the first day of our holidays. We had slept overnight in the car. Leaving the lay-by early the next morning, we headed south. I sat in the front passenger seat; Tom was dozing in the back and Hugh was driving. I have no memory of the crash. Apparently, the car travelling in the opposite direction, crossed the road and smashed head-on into us. Both cars were minced! Sailing through the windscreen was ok, with my looks, anything would be an improvement, but the cerebral haematoma was unfortunate. I was unconscious for a few days, but as they wheeled me down for surgery, I thankfully regained consciousness and was taken back to my bed. The haematoma had dissolved! Periods of unconsciousness were still occurring though not for so long or so deeply. The headaches were horrendous!

Sleeping on duty was a sackable offence. Telling the truth seemed the only option, but because I had failed to mention it at my interview, the bright lights of the job centre beckoned me with my P45! It was dawn. The sky was unsure, whether to let the sun rise or create eternal night. Gazing out the window, I froze at the terrifying screams coming from the courtyard. What on earth was happening? The quiet, half-light intensified my mounting dread, then it uttered the high-pitched scream again! My eyes widened, as I searched the dark corners. It strode confidently across the tarmac, the many eyes blazing with fury! The peacock was commanding the sun, and everyone else, to awaken! I had discovered the reason for the local horror stories!

All the day staff knew about it, they were very supportive? "Franken hates mental nurses, she has sacked them for the least thing. You may as well leave now". She had worked in a general hospital as a ward sister, before deciding that the mentally ill were more in need of her 'tender loving care'? Her reputation would indicate that she considered us inferior to general trained nurses. It did not look good!

"You were sleeping last night, putting your patients at risk". Her mouth was two thin lines that shot the words into the pit of my stomach. "Your reason for sleeping on duty should have been discussed at your interview." Staring out the butterfly design on the carpet, I waited to hear the inevitable. She continued. "I see from your records that you have a sister. As it happens, your sister and I trained and worked together, she is an excellent nurse, maybe you will follow her example. Return to your ward, I never want to hear another complaint regarding your conduct!"

I had survived the unmentionable; future night shifts would see me splashing my face with ice-cold water, drinking buckets of strong tea and regularly checking the patients. I still, at times, lapsed into a sleep, but was able to rouse myself at the least sound.

The ward staff were amazed, but even more so, when I told them that we had a great chat and she had invited me round for tea, when I was refreshed!

'Vee Ward', stood out like a green and white pavilion, overlooking the golf course. Although it was only a hundred yards from the main hospital, it was run like a cottage hospital. A geriatric unit, with twenty patients, 'Sister Saint' controlled it with a fist of iron! Dictatorial, fearsome and unbending, she was nevertheless totally devoted to her patients and if they fitted in with her high standards, the staff were also privileged to accept her benevolence. With the office sitting in the middle, to the left, ten female beds, to the right, ten male beds. All the patients were hand picked by Sister Saint, for they were required to be quiet, settled and docile, with a long history of good behaviour. In the event that, heaven forbid, a patient should become restless or behave badly, then they would be rapidly, transferred back to the main hospital. There was always a waiting list of suitable candidates and no one in their right mind would dare to question any decision by this self-appointed 'Angel of Mercy'! It was rumoured, that she had been offered the post of matron, but when she said that half the directors on the board were criminals, it was considered preferable to leave her be.

This was a busy ward during the day. Helping patients to rise, bathing, changing, dressing, serving breakfast, doctor's rounds, medicine rounds and writing the ward report. The sister ensured the smooth running of the ward with two qualified and two assistant nurses. The afternoon shift was less frenetic, but the best shift was night shift! Once the day staff gave their handover report and went home, the patients were tucked up in bed, after being given their night sedation. The most frequently prescribed medication for psycho-geriatric patients were, Lactulose and senna, for their bowels, next came antacids, then Mandrax and Nitrazapam, which were mild sedatives. One lad with bowel cancer was prescribed ten millilitres of 'Brompton Cocktail', a mixture of opiates with effective pain relieving qualities!

'Night shift' then had a cup of tea with toast, sat and watched television or had some shuteye! The night superintendent usually came by at one in the morning, but this was not a problem, as the rattle of the key in the door, would waken the dead! In the event of a wet night, he would simply phone over for a report.

Nursing assistant 'Flusey' and male staff nurse 'Chickweed', were the regular staff on night shift. She was a troubled soul, and looked to be past her 'sell by' date! With too much makeup and dressed in her daughters gear, for all that, she was a worker and fussed over the patients like a mother hen. In contrast, staff nurse 'Chickweed', was quiet and dour. His black eyes never betrayed a flicker of emotion or compassion. Trying to speak to him was like drawing teeth. Stout and tall, with grey hair, he seemed a cross between a slug and an owl! Everyone thought that he must be related to sister Saint, as this seemed the only explanation for employing this excuse for a nurse!

'Chic' went off sick. Hopefully, he had booked into a private clinic, for a personality transplant! In his place, we were blessed with staff nurse, Mickey Tack. "It's good to see you again, Flusey. I would give you a hug, but I'm not into necrophilia!" His humour was always at someone's expense. Good looking, in a garish sort of way, he was too thin and too ingratiating. When he laughed at his own jokes, he would give a sickening cough that made you wince!

Night shifts were uneventful, apart from the cancer patient becoming restless and moaning day and night? Sister Saint was baffled, so the doctor was ordered to attend and he could only guess that the patient had become accustomed to his medicine and increased the dose by five millilitres per dose. The moaning continued! Mickey went on holiday, for a fortnight and his stand-in, wee Jimmie struggled to cope with the change from 'ordinary' staff nurse, to 'elite' Vee ward, staff. During this time, the bottle of Brompton Cocktail was used up and a new bottle was ordered from the pharmacy. After the drug round that night, the staff realized that something was missing? There was silence! Not a moan to be heard. Was he dead? He was sleeping like a baby! He slept that way for two days! The doctor was again summoned. The dose was reduced to the previous level and everything was back to 'normal'.

Sister Saint had no doubt about what had happened. When Mickey returned from holiday, she confronted him with the awful truth! "I know that you have been watering down the bottle of morphine! What you did with it is your problem and though we are unable to prove what you did, I will ensure that you are never left in charge of a ward". Mickey never met her flaming stare, nor did he attempt to deny his crime. "You will return to the main hospital and the matron will allocate your duties". He eventually moved on to greater things, at another hospital!

There were many characters spread over the hospital. 'Forty Pockets' would go round all the wards selling newspapers. The money would go into different pockets for different coins. You not only had to check your change; you needed to check the date on the paper, as it was often out of date! "This is yesterday's paper!" Never a flicker of emotion, "I just sell the papers, doesn't mater what date is on them". So saying, he would lumber on to his next customer.

'Boon' had been born that way. Bent forward almost double, his hands dragging on the floor, made it difficult for him to stand. They called him, 'Monkey's Miscarriage'. He had to run to keep from falling over on his face. To get anywhere, he had to head for a chair, and grab onto it to stop himself falling. If he misjudged the distance, he would run out of breath, have to stop and would fall on his face. His one redeeming feature was his photographic memory. He knew everybody's name, age and where they were from. He loved when one of the women would take pity on him and take his hand to support him. This didn't last, as he would frequently fall over and grab them by their breasts, to steady himself. He tended to fall more often when he had a female holding him up! 'Torn-hole' had once been a terrible alcoholic. His reaction to booze was particularly severe. He would simply go berserk! Many injections of Paraldehyde were required in his buttocks, to settle him down. The problem was that the injections were corrosive, burning the flesh from his cheeks. It took months of bed rest and sugar poultices, to heal the gaping holes. Physically weak and mentally impaired, Torn-hole, spent the rest of his days in hospital, where he would brush the ward floor, wax and polish, then arrange the furniture, all before the doctors round, at ten o'clock. During all this, he would shout at the patients for being so lazy. Some of them would respond and wind him up; by saying they were tired after being out with his wife all night! Tornhole, would shout and scream all manner of abuse, at this 'alley cat'. After a few minutes, it was all forgotten and he would go and wash the breakfast dishes and tidy the kitchen.

Every Thursday, 'Skybo' would collect his pay for ward duties, collect his pension from the Post Office, then walk quickly to the wood behind the hospital and deposit all the money into a tree trunk! He was very careful that he was not being followed, as there were many who tried. In later life, he would go up to the wood and realize that he had lost the tree trunk! The money was never found, at least no one admitted to finding it!

Problem Child

Becoming increasingly confused, stagnated and numbed by my job and lack of progress, I felt it was time for some 'self discovery'. I have never been ambitious, in fact, usually very contented and settled. So what the hell was my problem now? I sensed that because things were so pleasant and undemanding, the alarm bells were clanging. Perhaps there was the similarity between how things were at the moment and the time at the sweet factory just before it closed. I was doing a job I enjoyed, that didn't stretch my imagination or ability. Everything was so good and it felt comfortable and safe, then, bang, it was all gone! Out of the blue, I would be on the dole, suffering all manner of depression and anxiety. Could it possibly be a throwback to my childhood, causing me to react in this way? My insecurity at home, waiting in the rain till the arguments settled, before I could sneak in to my bed. The hungry nights, when there were no apples on the trees, or the bullying and feelings of inferiority at school.

The time had come, for me to assume the roll of client! She was, or claimed to be, a qualified hypnotherapist, with funny letters after her name and a nice address. I was impressed enough to make an appointment for a, 'mind examination'. At the first session all my personal details were extracted, all my expectations were either confirmed or destroyed. 'May I smoke during our session?' 'No'. 'Will I remember everything that I say?' 'Yes'. 'May I phone you to ask about something that may come to mind?' 'No. Keep it for your next session'. I was also informed, that it was my responsibility to make the most of my session. Ten sessions, one a month, were all I could afford, although it seemed that I could go on forever, discovering different facets of my personality.

Each session started with reflections on the material from the previous session. Then my current thoughts were explored and examined, finally, the bit I liked best, deep relaxation with ventilation of feelings emerging from the previous thirty minutes. Although it was enjoyable, the format seemed to be 'written in stone' with any investigation of uncomfortable feelings disregarded, leaving me a trifle disillusioned and disappointed, much like my feelings toward my family. Nevertheless, it was an opening up of my self-knowledge and had been instrumental in helping me find a way forward. It would appear that my bad feelings associated with my upbringing have left me with a simmering undercurrent of anger and aggression; consequently, I blamed my mother for all my problems in life; rationalization had come to my rescue! At least I was more aware of my problems, but, what could I do to resolve them?

Having finished using the toilet, I pulled out the white sheet of toilet roll, again, that familiar fear flashed through my mind, like the flushing of a putrid toilet bowl. For goodness sake, I had only been eight years old when it happened! His voice was rancid with hate, "Now I've got you. You're the one that's been pulling all the paper off the rolls. Look at the mess in here. You thought you would get away with it again!" Grabbing me by my jacket collar, he hauled me out It was only then that I noticed, that in my rush to get on the toilet, I had failed to notice the miles of streamers, strewn across the floor, brightening up the dull grey, concrete ablutions.

Dragging me, unceremoniously, through the screaming schoolchildren in the playground, the janitor bundled me through the door marked, 'Headmaster'. "Sit on that bench, while I see what your headmaster has to say about your destructive behaviour". As I sat shivering in the waiting room, I listened to the indistinct voices and wondered what was happening. My first week in school and already my promising academic career was in the balance!

"Come into my office, boy". The headmaster growled, as the janitor marched proudly out the door, another master criminal brought to justice. I stared up at the mountain of lard. "Why did you destroy all the toilet rolls"? His malevolent stare did nothing for my confidence. "I didn't do anything, sir". "You were caught red-handed, boy, so you will have to receive six of the belt, now hold out your hands". The sheer injustice of my situation was magnified by my mixed emotions of hurt and anger. "No, I did nothing wrong". His eyes narrowed. "Sit outside, boy". After an eternal five minutes, I was amazed to see my sister sidle into the headmaster's office. Another eternity crept by. "Come into the office, boy, and listen to your sister". She looked stern and her voice sounded alien! "Please accept your punishment for what you did". There was no argument. I took the belt, but I would never forget the lesson, 'don't get caught'! To this day, when I go to use the toilet roll, my mind flashes back to that terrible injustice and I feel the same hurt and anger.

It is my opinion that sometimes a problem, should be left alone, as it can provide a driving force that keeps us motivated, a source of determination or obstinacy, and an inbuilt safety device. Without it we may lose our way, become stagnated or lack a sense of purpose in life. Am I simply making excuses for the therapists' incompetence? A potential client asked me to cure her fear of spiders, as she lived in Australia it was not a good idea to forget that many spiders there are particularly poisonous. So perhaps the customer is not always right.

Non-Person

"My lodger gets on to me for being too soft, not going out enough, wearing dowdy clothes and then demands a reduction in her rent!"

Jazmine was going over the same scenario once again. She was a plain, middle-aged lady, who had been 'knocked back' too many times. Nursing her mother and father, till they both died, then for her live-in boyfriend to disappear, with most of her savings, had left her with a smouldering depression.

"Why don't you join a dance club?"

"Not with my two left feet, anyway, I get dizzy when I turn too quickly and I would be too embarrassed. The very thought makes me burst out in goose pimples". It was like a fencing match, only 'touché' was not in her vocabulary.

Jazmine, was delighted with her therapy sessions, although there was no real improvement in her underlying condition. She was happy to talk to somebody who listened and didn't put her down all the time. She was the therapists dream client, eager to listen, keen to agree, never asked too many questions and paid without a grumble. Her last therapist was quickly ditched, when he started consulting the 'tea leaves'. But my conscience was starting to give me a hard time. There had to be a way to stop her co-dependence, lift her mood and self-esteem, but what? I decided to give her a specific task that would challenge her 'belief system'. "What do you think would happen if you said to your lodger, 'the rent has to rise by ten percent'?"

"She would probably slap me across the face then move out".

After a lot of haggling, cajoling and support, she agreed to type an 'official' letter stating the new rent increase! The next appointment was in a week's time. I wished her luck and crossed my fingers.

Jazmine looked very worried as she shuffled into the consulting chair. "Well, how did you get on with the lodger?" My fingers were still crossed. "It went fine. She has agreed to pay the new rent, but I feel I've let her down somehow".

"In what way do you feel that you have let her down?"

"Well, she looked deflated, beaten! I feel guilty. Maybe she won't like me now. It all seems to rebound on me."

"I wonder when you felt that feeling before. You may even have said the same words."

For a long time she appeared puzzled. Jazmine looked down and to her left. This meant that she was remembering her past and getting in touch with her feeling. Neuro-linguistic programming, teaches us, that most people look to their right, when thinking about the future, to their left, when remembering their past and down, when getting in touch with their feelings. As if a weight had been lifted from her shoulders, she exclaimed, "Your right!" I uncrossed my fingers.

"Mother and father made me feel the exact same way. Why would they do that?" Her face showed the mixed emotions that were coursing through her mind. "I feel embarrassed, used and angry, at the way my parents manipulated me. How could they do that?"

It took Jazmine several weeks, to work through the stages of, disbelief, sadness, anger, and then acceptance. It was explained that her parents may have been frightened that she would leave them. 'What will become of us, if our daughter abandons us?' She had also encouraged their dependence on her. The need to be wanted and loved is very powerful, though not always wise! Aaron. T. Beck pioneered Cognitive Behaviour therapy, which recognizes that if you change what you think, how you react, or deal with a situation, can determine the consequences or outcomes.

Medicine Mayhem.

A most enjoyable breakfast was washed down with a strong, hot cup of tea, coffee was not an option. The medicine trolley had been prepared, tablets and syrup in individual glasses, lined up in the order they were to be handed out. Largactil, Melleril and Lactulose syrups, Phenobarbitone, Sodium Amytal, Epanutin, Distalgesic, Tetracycline, Artane, Digoxin tablets and capsules and a host of medicinal miracles created a baffling array of all shapes and sizes, colours and smells. The patients lined up in an orderly queue, all hoping this time they would be cured!

Through the back, in the dormitory, Tobac was up to his usual tricks, pilfering from his fellow patients lockers! His eyes lit up as he spotted the half-ounce of tobacco that John. G had hidden under the vest in his locker. Just as he was throwing it into his jacket pocket, John, G appeared at the door having returned from the toilet where he had been washing himself in preparation for his garden job. Now you wouldn't say John G was big, no, you were more likely to describe him as massive! With a terrifying roar, he lunged toward Tobac, who had decided that the 'better part of valour', was to run very fast. This was no mean feat for Tobac as he was tall, ungainly and preferred to breathe in smoke rather than air. Lumbering between the beds and round the lockers, he dived down the corridor toward the sitting room cum dinning room. Cascading close behind him, John G was remarkably fast for a mountain of muscle! Tobac's long, lumbering strides, took him to the front of the queue, in a zigzag fashion. "Save me darling, there's a madman trying to kill me". Cappy, looked over the top of his medicine trolley in time to see John G crash into Tobac, but not in time to avoid the tangle of bodies and medicines as they toppled over the trolley to be covered in all manner of syrup, emulsions and tablets. The basin of warm soapy water and the water jug followed like a chaser! All the patients and staff looked on, dumbfounded. "Oh darling, look what we've done." John G ripped the packet of tobacco from his pocket and slapped him on the top of his head. The charge nurse strolled from his office and surveyed the colourful mural of disarray, with eyes that had seen it all before. "Come on lads, let's get this mess cleaned up and have our breakfast in peace." Shaking his grey head, he returned to his mug of tea and bacon rolls.

The patient's were given their medicine from the medicine stock in the cupboard, which was so well stocked it would have been enough to supply the troops, in the event of war! The multitude of tablets and capsules strew across the floor were picked up and flushed down the toilet, the syrup and emulsions were mopped up, while the medicine trolley was scrubbed and disinfected, then restocked. Dangerous drugs, such as phenobarbitone and sodium Amytal, were counted and marked as destroyed then re-ordered from the pharmacy. Future drug rounds would see two staff nurses issuing the tablets and syrup to each patient as they arrived at the trolley then signed for in the drug kardex. The dormitory would be emptied and the door locked. It took longer to organize but it was safer!

"Will you stop coughing in my face? Cover your mouth and put that fag away, you can hardly smoke for wheezing!" My complaint was drowned in another bout of uncontrollable coughing and spluttering. The ward had asked the duty doctor to take a look at Donque, due to his episodes of gasping for breath and night sweats, his temperature went up and down all night? His face was a ghastly white with absurd red patches high on his cheekbones, which was reminiscent of a clown. His breathing was laboured and he complained that, 'The devils stabbing me in the chest'. It must surely be a case of heavy smoking with a chest infection. It didn't stop him dragging deeply on his cigarette and coughing up specks of blood!

Unfortunately, this thirty-year-old lad could not explain his symptoms, for long ago he had withdrawn from the harsh world of reality and replaced it with all kinds of hallucinations and delusions. It was heart rending to watch him struggle with his internal hell, his reality, an emotional maelstrom of contradictions that made no sense to anyone, least of all, himself! One moment he would be laughing and singing, the next crying and screaming. It was not unusual for Donque to run up to you, putting his face right in front of you. "It's going to happen, you know, I can hear them whispering their plans to destroy the world!" Then he would run to his chair and curl up, in the foetal position. Were it not for the powerful antipsychotic and tranquilizer drugs, he would be very dangerous.

The duty doctor put him on a five-day course of antibiotic and as required, decongestant cough mixture. "Just keep an eye on him and take his temperature every hour, through the night". We gave him a bath and put warm clothes on him. He never left the ward, never watched television, listened to the radio or even a record. Meals were picked at, like a sparrow and he would only drink milk!

Off course, dominoes were not our only diversion when the charge nurse was off and the ward was quiet. Late afternoon, before supper, evenings and nightshift were good times for our other favourite game; cribbage! This game is attributed to Sir John Suckling, and is played by two, three or four players. Double players can also play it. Playing cards are dealt and pegs placed in holes on a board to keep the score. A point for each hole and thirty-one points is the winning score. Bets are placed, that when one is finished the rest pay, depending on how many holes they are from the finish. Normally we played for a penny a hole, but some would bet as much as a pound a hole! The game was so popular; one ward had the holes drilled into a dinning room table, to facilitate speed when setting up the game!

The 'Château', a locked ward, was crescent shaped with a five-foot high iron railing across the front. This ward had a diverse population. There were a few children; one was a hermaphrodite, having both male and female organs! Young and old men, ranging in diagnosis from paranoia, alcoholism, confusion, mental deficiency to sexual deviation, also inhabited this unusual mix of humanoids! On a summers day they would all sit out in the front compound playing and chatting. Despite the crazy mish-mash of problems, they all got on remarkably well. One patient, he was nicknamed Pokey, had appeared in court charged with bestiality. 'How do you plead?' the judge demanded. 'Well, it was like this, your honour. On the evening in question, I had imbibed of a considerable quantity of intoxicating refreshment. On passing adjacent to a quiet meadow, suddenly, the need to relieve my bladder was apparent so I climbed over into the greenery and began to relieve the pressure. Unbeknown to me, at this moment, a cow backed its hindquarters onto my copulatory organ!' At this point, the court was erupting into hysterics and Pokey was referred to us for assessment!

But it was Quaid, who was the star turn, or as he preferred to be addressed, Queeny? He/she was a transvestite, with a confused gender identity. He was determined to become a woman, but the only way to achieve this was to dress as a woman and take female hormone tablets for a year! After this time, he might be put on the waiting list for a sex-change operation! Queeny, hardly slept, so he decided to use his time wisely? He spent most nights teaching me the beautifully skilled, tactical and strategic allegory of war! I would learn to play Chess!

Quaids problem would seem to stem from incongruity between anatomic sex and gender identity. Before this can be diagnosed, there needs to be at least two years evidence of the disturbance! Often they have identity problems as children and it is more common in males, who may wish to be rid of ones genitals and live as a member of the other sex.

Pokeys habit of using animals as a preferred method of achieving sexual excitement, is labelled Zoophilia. Usually the individual prefers an animal that they had contact with during childhood.

Pervert Percy.

The bus station was busy. A mother was struggling to get off the bus with her four-month-old, howling daughter and an obstinate pram.

"Let me hold your baby, while you get the pram". The gentleman's voice was kind and soft. Clean, immaculate hands reached out for the child.

'What a nice gentleman', thought the mother as she handed the baby into his open arms. "Thank you". She turned to wrench the pram free and winced at the child's 'spoilt' screams. Arranging the blankets, she tucked the still screaming brat into the pram and hurried away. "Thank you so much".

The mother would not have been so grateful, had she checked her daughters' private parts and noticed the bruising, inflicted by his probing fingers! He smiled to himself as he savoured the excitement, coursing through his genitalia and looked for his next victim.

In his army days, as a sergeant stationed in India, a few rupee's would ensure a steady supply of very young children to his tent, the only prerequisite being, they must have no hair whatsoever on their private parts! On his demob, he returned to live with his sister and her three children. When she eventually realised that he was using her children for his sinister purposes, she reported him to the police. Percy, was admitted, through the courts, for, treatment?

He was prescribed medication, that stopped the production of sperm, a form of chemical castration. He was also required to convince the psychiatrist that he would not re-offend.

The man was a real horror! During our many chats, it was blatantly obvious that he had no intention of changing. "I just do my time, tell the medic's what they want to hear, then its back to 'kiddy sex' with a vengeance!" He often lashed out at staff or patients. When challenged about his behaviour, he would tell the doctor, 'He called me a pervert' or 'They spat on my food'.

Some months after his discharge, he was discovered in his flat. He had been dead for some time. A cerebral haemorrhage! Maybe there is a God!

"Will you escort a patient from the airport to the infirmary and stay with him for the rest of the shift?" It was always' great to do something away from the hospital. The ambulance picked me up and we waited for the plane to land. The ambulance crew told me that the patient would be sedated, as he was very violent and did not want to go into hospital for the removal of an ingrown toenail. The small plane landed and the doors opened.

Helping to take the stretcher off the plane, I saw that the unconscious man was small but stocky, almost square! I was handed a plastic bag that had a tube running into a vein in his arm. "That is Heminevrin in the drip, maintain a steady rate of twenty drops per minute. If he starts to become restless, increase it to thirty drops a minute, then reduce again when settled". Without a further word, the doctor returned to the plane and we were on our own! 'What the hell do we have here? He must be very dangerous if he needs to be knocked out to attend surgery!' The drip was a powerful hypnotic. It was normally used for patients withdrawing from alcohol. It could only be used short term, as it was very addictive!

At the Infirmary he was transferred onto a bed, a stand was positioned to hold the drip, which was running low, the doctor said she would return later to replace it. I kept a wary eye on all his vitals, temperature, pulse, respirations and blood pressure. A couple of times he stirred and threatened to waken, I immediately increased the flow of the drip and was amazed to see him rapidly sink back into inertia, then returned the drip to normal. This was a great number. No worries!

The doctor returned with a fresh bag of Heminevrin. Closing the valve that regulates the flow, she removed the empty bag and connected up the full one. Opening the valve, she set the number of drips per minute. Without a word, she sped out of the ward. It was all so fast and looked so efficient, I wondered had I imagined it! Looking back at the patient, I was horrified to see his body suddenly collapse into itself. Everything was defunct! The patient was dead! Glancing at the drip, I realized that the valve had released and was fully open; the drug was simply pouring into his body! Closing the valve completely, I pressed the emergency bell.

I had often thought that these bells were simply there to instil a false sense of confidence, and in fact were not even connected! Imagine my surprise therefore, when seconds later, a team of doctors and nurses rushed in with an emergency trolley. Electrodes were placed on the chest, 'stand back', the body arched, oxygen was administered and injections were given. Then they left, as suddenly as they had arrived.

The drip had been regulated to twenty drops per minute; his breathing, pulse and blood pressure were normal. Everything was once again settled and peaceful. It was with some relief that I handed over a living patient to the nurse on night shift!

Time Management.

All the patients were quiet and still. No admissions or transfers, no staff on holiday and only the long-term sickies, with chronic fatigue and pregnancy. Further study of the ward off duty sheet was fruitless; there was no chance of any overtime! Other wards were just as quiet. Something had to be done, so that we could get overtime! But what could be done? As things stood we would have to spend time at home with the wife and kids, you would just get under their feet and wonder what to do with yourself.

Something drastic had to be done! It was time to get the little grey cells working. George was normally a quiet, pleasant kind of guy, that was until it was mentioned that some of the more feminine patients had expressed an interest in him! Or maybe, Harry! Always a time bomb that was threatening to explode. Now, if daft Davy were to whisper in his ear that he had slept with his wife, last night, all hell would break loose and it would need four nurses to restrain him, for at least twelve hours! There were a couple of other patients that could be, 'wound up', but they usually took longer to react.

'Sicknote' was a senior staff nurse with a problem; he was a hypochondriac! All of the shift, he would be studying himself in the mirror, checking that the spots on his face were not multiplying, or becoming infected. Were his eyelids too white? Did his gums seem swollen? He would take his temperature, check his pulse, ask another staff nurse, or better still a doctor, to record his blood pressure. Was his urine and faeces dark? Perhaps a sign, of internal haemorrhaging! His fingertips were tender due to all the pinpricks for blood, as he checked for glucose, ketones, or a raised white blood cell count, a sure sign of infection! By simply mentioning to Sicknote that he looked 'under the weather', he was guaranteed to go off sick for a week!

Big Is Beautiful.

I had agreed to give the sisters a joint session. It was not to be my most sagacious decision. The 'slender eating plan', seemed a reasonable technique, to address their combined weight problem of forty-five stone!

The chairs screamed in protest, as they sat down, seemingly unaware of my terror, at the thought of them claiming vast sums from my indemnity insurance for injuries received from the two broken chairs.

"The rationale for this method is the need to get back in touch with your stomach. Usually we eat food, without acknowledging the messages from our digestive system".

They looked at each other, then at me. For one horrible moment, I thought they might break into song! "What is the success rate for this method?"

Were they investigators for some organisation, I wondered?

"If you follow the plan, it is inevitable that you will lose weight. How much, depends on you. Statistics are not available at this time due to the many, multifaceted indeterminables". Again, they looked at each other and seemed to acquiesce.

After a rapid relaxation, they were instructed on how to be 'at one' with their stomach's. We then ran through the process of eating. Seeing the food on a plate in front of you, then putting it in your mouth, chewing it, tasting the full flavour as it mixes with your saliva. Now swallow the food and feel it slide down into the stomach, feel how your stomach feels as the food lies there. "Before eating or drinking anything, you must first run it through this process in your mind, then, decide if you really wish to eat it. Most times, you will realize that you have no need to".

People normally find that they feel satisfied after doing this procedure. It is explained, that after several days, the mind will run the sequence automatically, in a split second, whenever they see food or drink.

For the umpteenth time they seemed to exchange opinions, telepathically.

"We realize that this is not what we expected". Her huge green eyes looked through me, searching for an answer.

"What did you expect?" Should I have asked this question earlier?

"We thought there would be massage, exercises and diet plans, you know, Calorie counting and all that".

I referred them on to 'weighty watchers' and ushered them quickly out the door. My need for clients, was clearly outweighing, (no pun intended.) my clinical judgement. It was not to be my last error!

Eighteen Eighty-two.

Donques' cough refused to clear up. The hourly temperature, at night, showed steps up and down on the graph, as his body heat fluctuated! The duty doctor ordered a sputum sample, to be sent to the bacteriology department. Two days later another sample was sent, then a third sample! A week later, with no improvement, all the staff were called to the ward office. The consultant and the duty doctor were already there, along with the charge nurse and the nursing officer. The consultant spoke. "It would seem that we have a case of, Tuberculosis, in the ward". We all looked at each other and gave a nervous cough; at least we hoped it was merely a nervous cough! "In order to avoid the infection spreading, it will be necessary to confine all patients to the ward and other measures will be implemented as required". Again, we looked at each other, wondering what, if any, were the ominous implications of 'other measures'. We were informed, after the doctors left, of these 'other measures'! Only the current staff would be allowed to work in this ward; everyone would require to have, an x-ray and a mantoux test, white coats to be worn at all times and sent to the laundry under 'infected wash'. The good news was that we would be required to cover the overtime, as no staff from other wards, could be allowed to enter this ward!

All our patients would be x-rayed and given a mantoux test. They would also be required to supply a sample of sputum, on three consecutive days. In the event that anyone was found to be infected, like Donque, they would be given streptomycin, isoniazid and para-aminosalicylic acid. The mantoux test consists of a dead protein of the tuberculosis bacilli injected under the skin. An inflamed, or positive reaction indicates previous exposure to the bacilli. This was first recognised by, Robert Koch, in 1882, and for his work on this and cholera, anthrax, bubonic plague and malaria he was awarded a Nobel Prize, in 1905.

The next couple of weeks were the busiest in all our lives. Obtaining dozens of sputum specimens, blood and urine specimens, labelling them and then sending them to bacteriology, haematology and microbiology. Escorting all the patients to the x-ray unit, which was parked at the side door, then, getting our own photos taken. It became easier as we got used to all the different procedures of barrier nursing, hygiene and filling in all the different forms for the various departments.

Most of the patients and staff smoked, though some did manage to kick the habit. I stopped for a whole two weeks! We all invented a host of reasons, why we could not or would not stop. "I get a terrible cough when I stop." "My doctor told me not to do anything suddenly." "Only the good die young." "Don't be a silly, wee man. How can I possibly be affected when I'm an alien?"

Donque, was continuing to deteriorate, so he was due to be transferred to the 'Fevers' ward at the general hospital. Sadly, he died, that night and the seriousness of the disease, was hammered home. Over the next two months, more and more sputum results were returned, with a negative result, on all three samples. One patient, who continued to be positive, was transferred to the isolation ward, where he remained for a further three months!

At the present time, Tuberculosis kills two million people each year, mostly in developing countries!

The Box

The story goes that a doctor-cum-farmer was sitting watching his dog run about the room. This dog was as mad as a March hare! It never stood still and had a temper like a bull with a migraine! When the dog tripped over a wire, it turned and sank its teeth into the cable. It went stiff as the electricity shot through its body. To the doctor-cum-farmers' surprise, the dog became settled and docile? It was to be the first example of Electro-convulsive Therapy!

E.C.T. day was upon us! The spare nurses, around the hospital, were ordered to go to the department, wearing clean white coats, at eight forty-five. Meantime, the charge nurse at the department was preparing for the thirty or so patients that were to be 'cured'! The trolleys were made up with clean, crisp sheets and lined up in the corridor outside the waiting room. Screens, were strategically placed, to afford some privacy. He would then wash his hands in a mixture of water and dettol! Rubber mouth gags, to place between the teeth, were laid in a neat row, hands were washed again. Emergency equipment, oxygen, resuscitation tray, suction machine, and cardiac restart machine. Again, hands washed! The E.C.T. Box, was plugged in and checked. A similar department, at another hospital, had their E.C.T. box tested and it was discovered, that it was 'dead'! The patients were not getting any electrical shocks! There was no apparent difference noticed in the effect of treatment when the 'box' was functioning and when it wasn't? 'Dettol Donnie' washed his, red raw, hands again and braced himself for the onslaught!

Patients, who were due for treatment, were allowed to stay in bed because they were not allowed breakfast. A plastic strap, with their name and ward, was fastened to their wrist. Before marching down to the department, they would be taken to the toilet to empty their bladders! As we walked along the corridor, other patients with staff, would filter in, making a strangely quiet pilgrimage to the Promised Land?

We all sat in the waiting room, until our patients' name was called. Some patients would be shivering in anticipation, remembering the small butterfly needle jabbed into a vein at the arm, then taped down. The cold injection and the panic as the muscle relaxant and anaesthetic kicked in; they were unable to breathe, move or speak, sometimes they would wet themselves! The oxygen mask was slapped over their mouth, then, blessed unconsciousness! After a couple of lungfuls of oxygen, the rubber gag was inserted, between the teeth or gums, electrodes were placed at each side of the temples. The three nurses around the trolley, were instructed to firmly hold the shoulders and knees. The doctor would check the patients' notes, to see the previous amount of joules used and if this produced a satisfactory seizure. The correct power would be set and the button pressed! The body went rigid for a few seconds before the rhythmical jerking began. Usually after a couple of minutes they would settle, the gag removed, an airway pressed down over the tongue and more oxygen administered. When the patient started to regain consciousness, he or she, would be turned onto their left side; the side rails put in position and wheeled through to the recovery ward?

The patient was allowed a few minutes of sleep as the butterfly needle and airway were removed. Pushed and prodded, they were reminded that they had received treatment and that it was all over. As they awakened, confused and bewildered, their socks and slippers were put on; they were sat up and put into a dressing gown, then whipped onto a wheelchair. Racing back to their ward, they were again reminded that treatment was over and they could now enjoy a cup of tea and a bacon roll!

Soldier Donald's mother came up to see him every second day. A pathetic sight as they paced up and down the ward, his mother trying to instil some confidence into his brain. The drugs, on their own and in combination did not seem to have any effect, as did the numerous sets of electro-convulsive therapy! Still confused, frightened and depressed, he was a very sorry sight! To add to his problems, he was losing weight and had developed a chesty cough! It was therefore decided, that since the medicine did nothing for him, all treatment was to cease! This was radical psychiatry indeed! We all looked on, with bated breath, over the next few months.

At first, Donald seemed to sink even further into himself, perhaps thinking that even the medical staff had given up on him! Then slowly, but surely, he began to surface. His appetite improved, he started to look after himself better. When his mother was due to visit, he would wash and dress smartly? Even a smile was to be seen, on rare occasions! He was able to go home for weekends. Finally, he was discharged and would be seen up the town, happily doing the shopping with his mother on his arm.

A Shining Example.

As in every community there were a few 'bright lights' that seemed destined to reach high office and indeed some of them did well. Everything they do seems perfect, everything about them emanates success. You wonder if it would rub onto yourself if you touched them?

These people can latch onto patterns of probability, using them to predict answers and are able to rapidly process variations within these patterns. Their expanded consciousness and wide perceptive area creates enormous comprehension with awesome speed of thought, much like a trillion K computer on triple broadband!

Black wavy hair that shone healthily, light brown eyes, straight, slender nostrils crowning a petulant mouth, with a strong determined jaw. The body, under the white starched coat, was bronzed and machine tooled. No, it was not Adonis; it was 'Sam the sham'!

This idyllic creature was the shining light of the hospital. He had shot through all his exams, gaining a 'First', for his outstanding results. This staff nurse was destined for great things! Management would have him escorting dignitaries around the hospital, on their rare visits. Meetings of any importance would be chaired by this 'iconic perfection'. In his spare time he tutored some of the students and sang in the church choir.

Nobody really knew him; he was a very private person. When he spoke, in his silky, well-modulated voice, it was as if you were receiving a lecture. Even the students he taught would never say anything about him? He stayed in the nurses' home, at the top flat.

I was speaking to b.b. (babe bait.) He proudly informed me that he had a steady girlfriend. Her name was Anora! She had been admitted a week ago and apart from her poor appetite, she was going to be fine. They seemed well suited and were together at every opportunity. They were inseparable. I found out that she did have an eating problem; it was called 'anorexia'!

Doda, came running out of the toilet, terror was etched into his face and wide eyes as he crashed into me. "What's the problem?" He trembled, as he looked over his shoulder. "I was shaving and this monster appeared in the mirror. Do you think he will kill me?" Several other patients were at various stages of shaving, washing and dressing. "Let's go back to the mirror and find this monster". I countered, taking him firmly by the arm and leading him back to his mirror. He stared deeply into his own reflection.

Doda, was a young schizophrenic. Tall and slim, his sandy, tousled hair fell over a boyish face. His soft, white skin and long, thin fingers, gave a feminine impression and in fact, there were many times, when he would only wear women's clothes? "Allow yourself to see the monster now. You'll be safe with me beside you!" "Its there now. There it is!" His eyes went wide and body rigid. "OK. Try to imagine the monster with ears like Mickey Mouse! Now, see his neck stretch, just like a giraffes! The funny monster speaks and all you can hear is a squeak, like a mouse!" Doda, was now smiling and relaxed, obviously enjoying the transformation. "It's disappeared now. Must finish shaving and get my breakfast."

It was great, to be able to help Doda, tackle his demons. Sadly, because there was no consistency in the help given and other nurses were unable to use these interventions, it was doomed to be swallowed up by all his other demons. A half percent of the population, will develop this illness, in early adulthood. One third of them will only suffer one bout or episode. One third will recover well, between bouts, but the final third, have recurring bouts, with more lasting difficulties in their lives! The reason, may be, hereditary , biochemical, family situation, relationships or stress. So, whether the problem emanates from the chicken or the egg, this centuries old illness, remains an enigma.

The union chairman gave me the 'Health and Safety' manual. His name was 'Nowel Roules' and he seemed to know what the health service was up to even before they did! Sharp as a ninja blade, he could convince you that although it was night, in reality, it was day? He was a born negotiator, who could twist fact into fantasy. The management were simply there to do his bidding. Nowel didn't care what he said, as long as it achieved the desired outcome. Defending, member Sue, against a possible sacking, for unprofessional work practices? He accused the male members of the panel of being hypocrites, because they fancied her! "Just because she won't let you shag her, you decide to vent your sexual frustration on her". The case collapsed, never to be resuscitated! So it was to be, that overnight I became the 'Health and Safety Officer' for the entire area? At times, it was necessary to stand in for union representatives who were off sick or on holiday. Then I had to deal with members work problems. Duncan came to see me. They called him 'Dunk the Drunk', maybe because he was an alcoholic. Problem was, he also doubled as an enrolled nurse! "You've got to help me. I'm up in front of matron, for a disciplinary hearing. She wants me to leave nursing because of my problem, but I've cut it down to the odd pint, so surely they can't sack me when I'm trying so hard to help myself!" He seemed to be bravely holding back the tears.

We sidled into the matrons office, her hat seemed bigger than ever, perhaps because she was sitting down, looking as prim as a stack of bibles! Mr. Mortiman was glued by her side. "Thank you both for attending". She said, ushering us into small, hard chairs. "You have been asked to attend today, Duncan, because we feel it would be wise for you to leave the service, voluntarily, rather than being dismissed!" I suspected that Dunk was hanging onto the job, because if he were unemployed, he would surely drink himself into an early grave. "May I enquire, on what grounds do you propose to dismiss our member?" They both looked at me as though I had propositioned them. Mr. Mortiman found his voice first. "Are you not aware, that Duncan has a serious drink problem. He has also been reported missing from his ward on several occasions, by his charge nurse. He simply walks of the job and goes down to the Off License. Even his short-term memory has been affected, for he forgets to come back!" My brain tried to think of a clever defence, but alas! "I believe it is hospital policy, to treat employees with a drink problem, compassionately and offer them help with their problem". Would this be enough to delay the inevitable? The hat stood up. "Very well, we will refer Duncan to the Occupational Health. However, if there is no improvement in three months time, we will terminate his employment".

Closing the door quietly behind us, Duncan's manner seemed to switch from subservient to bolshie? "They're a right couple of shitheads, that two. Can't a working man have an occasional bevy without all this agro"? With rapid, short steps, he raced out the front entrance, dragging off his tie as he went and stuffing it into the pocket of his camel hair coat. "Are you coming down for a pint? All that bullshit has made me dry. Come on; we'll get plastered!" "But we're both on duty". I shouted. "We should get back to our wards and we need to talk about this Occupational Health option!" But he was out of earshot; he was also out of control!

High Time at the Top.

"What you thinking about dude? Working in this shit-hole, where you can't even get your supply of smarties on time. Now I've got people relying on me, and I have to make deliveries, so hurry along and inform 'Sunny Boy' that Mr. B. is ready to roll, before I lose my cool exterior!"

Jinny, who was the font of all gossip, stared down at the wee, double-breasted clad stand-in for 'Banana Man', with his varnished nails and flat, black greasy hair. "Just one moment SIR! I'll get him on the bleeper" He went to the switchboard, at the back of the office and contacted the duty consultant, who then called the police. Banana man was dragged from the building, wide eyed in disbelief, to the waiting panda car.

'Sunny Boy' was the nickname of one of the nursing officers, because he was always laughing and joking. When the police interrogated 'Banana Man', a local drug dealer and the hospital held it's internal investigation, it was discovered that there were a number of staff, not only nursing, who were supplying pills as if they were going out of fashion. It was a bad time for the hospital. The papers turned it into a front-page scandal. Nobody admitted to working at 'Druggies Paradise'!

He was adamant that his name was 'King Duncan', believing that he was heir to the Scottish throne! Every once in a while, he would decide that a woman he had met, should marry him and be his queen! Day and night, he would bombard her with his 'royal command'. She would receive letters, with a royal coat of arms, phone calls, flowers and presents, he would sit on her doorstep, even inform her parents and employer, of her intended betrothal! He was her shadow! Eventually, having failed to comply with the courts restraining orders, he would be readmitted to the hospital.

The only thing remarkable about this man, was his ability to get intoxicated, without any visible supply of alcohol? On returning from parole, he would be searched and breathalysed. Despite this and being observed at all times, he became more and more intoxicated as the evening wore on! "My subjects supply me with all my needs" he would respond, when asked. It was one of life's mysteries, which 'King Duncan' took to his grave!

Cappy, had reported his bike stolen! In truth, he had dumped it in the canal! The duty sergeant took him round the back of the police station, where recovered bikes were kept. "If your bike is there, just take it." The sergeants huge arm sweep over the sea of gleaming chrome. Pointing to a smart, sturdy bike, which was standing regally in the corner. "That's my bike there, thank goodness you found it!" As he stepped forward to wheel it away, he was coarsely grabbed by the collar and thrown out of the bike shed. Cappy, scurried away quickly, brushing the sparks that flew from his capstain full strength, from his jacket as the sergeant waved a huge fist. "That's my bike, you cheeky bugger! Don't let me catch you trying that trick again".

Executive Stress

It was early evening and she could hardly speak on the phone, as she threatened to become hysterical. "Please can I have an appointment now? I can't go on with my life feeling this way." Fortunately, I was free, so she was given directions and told to come right away. A very smartly dressed, sternly handsome, middle-aged woman rang the bell.

"I'm in charge of the allocation of finance to businesses, but my authority is always questioned by my immediate superior. It's a bloody nightmare! I really hate the bugger, but it is more than that; he seems to have some mysterious power over me. I get tongue-tied and cannot even look him in the eye. That's not me! I don't understand what is going on!"

There could be a number of reasons for her problem; is she paranoid? Psychotic? In love? Anxious? Or, is her boss the bugger she thinks he is? Perhaps, this is an existential crisis! The main thing that I had to keep in mind was that the client is the only one who can tell you! "Go over all the feelings you experience in this mans presence." At times, I had to guide her back on track, as she drifted onto unrelated problems. "You seem to be talking, not about your boss, but, about someone close to you. Can you think of someone else, to whom you had the same reaction?" Her eyes looked down to her hand-made shoes, then left, apparently having an internal conversation. Looking up at me, her smooth facial skin puckered up in a perplexed look. "I suppose, he could be like my father; blonde hair, moustache and the voice; harsh and critical!"

On further examination, it became apparent that what her boss was saying was quite reasonable, at times, even helpful, but because she had transferred her bad feelings for her father onto him, it felt as if she was a child again, being put down, belittled and controlled. Now that she understood her inappropriate reactions, relief, smoothed out her facial lines and she could appreciate that her boss was only doing his job!

A week later, I received a letter, thanking me for dealing with such a disturbed client and 'putting daddy in his place'.

Eastern Promise.

The patient had a high temperature; pulse and blood pressure were also raised and he was sweating profusely. Paracetamol was prescribed, to ease the discomfort and help lower his temperature. Cold compresses were applied and though regularly washed down, his temperature continued to soar. He passed away before we were informed that patients all over the hospital had suffered the same fate! Other hospitals reported a rise in fatalities, due to some kind of super-bug! Then it emerged that we were going to lose many more! It was an outbreak of Asian Flu!

It was winter and the old, weak and vulnerable were dropping like flies. Even the staff were hit and we had to work extra shifts to cover for them. When a patient died, we washed the body, shaved their face, placed cotton wool in their nose, mouth, ears and any other opening! We then tied the thumbs together over the chest and tied the ankles and big toes together with a label, stating name, date, time of death and ward and hospital number. Finally, a clean white sheet was wrapped around the body and taped in place. The bodies could only be shifted down to the mortuary, which was discreetly situated outside the hospital round the back, at nighttime, to avoid other patients being disturbed. The bodies would be put onto a gurney, a metal trolley with wheels, which had a metal, hinged cover. In the pitch dark of night, we would wheel the body through the snow and carry it into the mortuary. The bodies were piled high, one on top of the other. We were quickly running out of space.

This was a most unpleasant time. The only way to avoid getting depressed was to keep our spirits up with humour, no mater how inappropriate it seemed. On carefully placing a body on the mortuary slab, the nurse who was helping turned white, when the body groaned and sat up. The 'body' was actually a nurse, who thought it was a great idea to surprise his friend. His friend never spoke to him for months after! Ama Tird could not resist telling one of his offensive jokes. "What's the hardest part of a vegetable?" Even though we ignored him and continued drinking our tea, he persisted. "The coffin!" As he laughed loudly at his own joke and tears streamed from his eyes, he failed to notice the powdered laxative, being stirred into his sugary tea. "Drink your tea before you choke on the rubbish you talk". An hour and a half later he was unable to leave the toilet. It was a week before he returned to work!

It was two in the morning and another body was on the back road of the hospital, destined for the mortuary. The wind whipped the constant snow into our faces as we tried to rush through the drifting snow. Suddenly, the gurney swerved over the edge of the bank and rolled down the hill. With a superhuman effort, we dragged the gurney back onto the path and continued on our way. We lifted the cover off the gurney, to carry the body into the mortuary; to our horror, there was no body? The lid must have opened as it rolled down the hill and the body was left in the snow! We searched for ages, but it was an impossible task to find a white sheet in the dark and in the snow. We would resume our search in the daylight. Five of us walked through the snow at first light and eventually found the frozen corpse!

All good things come to an end and I guess that also holds for bad things. The numbers dying diminished rapidly and we returned to a semblance of normality. The many empty beds were a reminder of the epidemic, as if we needed one!

Know Thyself.

Sometimes, like when a client cancelled an appointment, I wondered why I bothered at all and I would ask myself, 'What had I done wrong?' Had I said something that put them off, or did they think that I would be unable to help them. Always I blamed myself. Quite apart from the self-flagellation, it meant wasted time and, dare I say, no money, as if that mattered! When someone phoned for an appointment, I would explain that their first session would involve information gathering; what was the problem, their desired outcome and we could then discuss various techniques and decide which was best for them. Finally, they would be taught a rapid relaxation technique, which would enhance their progress. A new client was a frightening prospect. Would they instantly dislike me, what if I couldn't help them! Were they psychotic, alcoholic, psychopathic? The worse client is a liar! It means going round in ever decreasing circles, until they are cornered into the truth. You have to let them face their demons in their own time. If they were not prepared for the truth, then they would simply adopt their particular defence mode.

Some rationalised the problem, making all manner of excuses for their behaviour, rejection may be used, 'It's not really a problem! Then there's denial, 'I don't want to talk about it'. An extreme defence would be a delusion. 'I'm fat because I don't eat enough'. This belief is not open to any logical argument, and is indicative of a fragile ego, or 'self'. The therapist should try to determine what supports the belief, why do they need that belief, what would be a more helpful way to think and how can it be achieved! Sometimes it is easier to talk about the problem, as if it belonged to someone else, so that they can distance themselves, feel safer and avoid the need for defensiveness. Defence mechanisms, are used to help us cope with problems we cannot handle. Neuroses can be a result of a breakdown in this mechanism.

Sometimes I feel so much sorrow, but it is too much and too deep for crying. Anyway, crying on my own achieves nothing, because I haven't changed anything. Something may change if I cried in company! They may ask, 'why are you crying?' but how do you explain a lifetime of hurt, disappointment and failure! They may comfort me and, once again, I have achieved a new low. Most would probably simply walk away. My real downers are the opportunities that I allowed to slip through my butterfingers. My old banger, it was the most popular car, in it's day, the Austin Ten. This would have been a great car to have today. The advance and retard settings, were set manually by a lever on the centre of the steering wheel. It was pure luck if the car started first time without backfiring and jarring your hand on the starting handle! There was a tiny motor, above the window, that ran the wiper. An engine, that purred like a sewing machine and had about the same power! The stamp and coin collection, which contained some impressive specimens, were swapped, for a pair of binoculars and comics! I have always regretted my inability to go to university, but school terrified me, with all these children, so noisy, full of themselves, so confident and cruel. The teachers were the worse bullies; shouting and ridiculing me, then I would get the strap for reasons that I failed to understand! Before I was due to leave for school, I would hide in one of our cupboards, or on the way to school, make a diversion to the swings, go for a long walk or, my favourite, go fishing at the harbour with ten feet of string, a hook and some worms. Many thoughtful hours were spent, sitting on the cold concrete steps longing for a big fish to bite, so that I could proudly take it home for supper. Those wasted years, when I should have been learning, can never be redeemed and so I had lost most of the basic fundamentals of knowledge in what should have been my formative years. By way of compensation, I decided to become a minimalist; any problems, are reduced to their fundamental level and hopefully then solvable. The mountain can seem so big and insurmountable, but if you walk up in easy steps, the view can be breathtaking. Every problem can be broken down into achievable chunks!

Three Bags Full.

This should be good; I was deemed fit to work in Daimien Lodge. This was a luxury department, housed in the mansion a few miles west of the main hospital. It was originally intended for patients with neurotic illnesses, but due to necessity was also used for alcoholics, with a need for discretion. Generally, these patients had either money, position, or were gifted individuals. Writers, entertainers, doctors, bored housewives and even consultant psychiatrists were treated here! These patients were fascinating to talk with, but they usually just wanted to hide away until they recovered. Our main jobs were to serve tea and meals, be discrete and remind them when they were due to attend therapies. These therapies consisted of electro-convulsive therapy, group work and occupational and art therapy. The main therapy was the 'games room'! Snooker billiards, darts, weights, punch-bag and dominoes. This was where we could talk freely, without the constraints of our economic, political, social or cultural differences.

We had the suspicion that one of the patients was drinking, but we could never find any evidence. It was when a domestic decided his room was a health hazard that the truth was revealed. As she hoovered the thick pile carpet, she banged into the wardrobe door, which sprung open, and she was covered in an avalanche of half bottles of whisky! Empty ones, of course! On his discharge, he ordered a taxi to the nearest pub!

The psychiatrist was, 'out of sorts', so it seemed a good time to sort out some of the malingerers, or Munchausen's syndrome. "We feel you are ready to be discharged home!" The patient looked up in horror. "But I feel so ill, I still suffer nightmares from the car crash…." Her voice, crisp and decisive, cut off his excuses. "It's out of our hands, perhaps your own family doctor can get you admitted to the main hospital. You will be discharged in two days time!" "Surely you couldn't be so unkind" He howled to her receding footsteps, his face as crimson as his cardigan.

The psychiatrist looked out her consulting room window onto the paved apron, bordering the grassy bank that merged so spectacularly with the forest beyond. 'I feel better already' she said to herself as she plotted her next momentous achievement. The body, dropping from the roof, marred her view, as it hurtled crimson and clumsily toward the paving, smashing silently, in his final grand gesture!

Suxanne was tall, plain and gangly with an intellect to match. As an enrolled nurse she functioned adequately, but she was devious and tended to push the boundaries of her 'job description'. When things were quiet in the evenings, she would go to the room of a newly admitted patient, would introduce herself as the duty doctor and inform them that a full physical examination was required. There was no discrimination, as both sexes received her full tender loving care. It was a long time before her extra-curriculum activities were uncovered. The reason being, Suxanne was very selective, only vulnerable patients were picked out for this 'special' treatment. She was rapidly transferred to the main hospital and, to avoid any publicity, it was all swept under the carpet. It was a very bumpy carpet!

It is as certain as night follows day, moon follows sun, or the inevitable cycle of nature! You come home from your shift, as you walk in the front door the phone rings. Your wife answers the phone and turns to look at you with pity in her eyes! "The ward is asking if you have the keys in your pocket?" There is a sudden awareness of the heavy bunch of ward keys, jangling in your coat pocket! "Damn it! Now I have to go all the way back with the bloody keys! Tell them

I'm on my way with them!" Exasperation is obvious, as the house shudders to the slamming door.

This is the second time this week that I have taken the keys home with me. I must be nuts! What is the night shift going to say this time? There has always been a problem between the shifts. When anything goes wrong, it is the 'other' shift that gets the blame!

"That patient seems upset! You would think the day shift would have sorted him out. He probably won't sleep tonight! More hassle." If a patient is difficult to rouse in the morning! "I bet the night staff poured his night sedation with a shaky hand! Typical of them, making sure they get a quiet night."

"You must love the job! You even take your work home". His impudent face puffed up with false pride. "Why don't you stay, see how the 'cream of nursing' work, you could pick up some handy tips!"

The 'Management' were constantly attempting to cut back the escalating cost of running the hospital. It was a constant battle between the unions, nursing officers, hospital management and 'National Health Service' accountants! The patients were the easy targets; their morning feast was reduced to a continental breakfast! Then they stopped supplying toothpaste, clothing and even the ambulance service were reluctant to ferry patients to hospital clinics! The nursing staff were then messed about. Our twelve-hour shifts were changed to eight-hour shifts. The unions fought back and a concession was reached to allow for extra charge nurses to be employed to cover the extra day shifts. Management got round this; by upgrading the deputy charge nurses and so reduced the outlay.

In order to prevent expense, charge nurses were not allowed to do overtime! Staff nurses would take charge of the ward on their days off. To cover the change in practice, nursing officers explained that it was necessary, to allow the staff to gain management experience. The final blow came when it was decided that charge nurses could only work on weekdays, nine to five!

Initially, all staff were paid fortnightly and we would line up to receive our pittance from the 'pay office' staff. This would take a long time because they would tell you what you were due, then proceed to count the money out onto the counter, which was placed in an envelope and you signed for it. Some years later we were granted weekly pay, which was much easier for us to manage, but it meant twice the work for the pay staff. In a bid to reduce the, pay office staff, all staff were requested to accept monthly pay, through there bank account? Most of us were allergic to banks, preferring to tuck any money we had left under our mattress. Permission slips were sent, in the pay envelope, to all staff to sign for acceptance of monthly pay! What most staff did not realize was that management could not force anyone to sign these slips. Consequently, as I refused to sign, it was many years before they finally found a way to make me accept monthly pay.

Back to School.

One day I would have to retire from nursing, so I had to think of something that would keep me busy and earn some money. My fascination for psychology and hypnosis dictated my choice. The answer was Hypnotherapy! Trouble with this was the time and astronomical cost of most of the worthwhile courses! I settled for a course that was being run at Glasgow. This was a three-year diploma qualification, which could be paid by instalments. By attending week-end classes, submitting essay's, that were marked externally and gaining certificates from seminars, I would be awarded their diploma, entered onto their national register and could even apply for membership of the 'British Association for Counselling'.

Having organised my weekends off work, which meant less pay, I happily drove the two hundred and odd miles to enter the world of 'the mind'!

a. There were twenty of us, from all walks of life. One fellow stated he was a 'spiritual healer' and declared that he had cured himself of cancer! Though I was dubious of his claim, he was interesting to listen to and seemed a well-bred gentleman. Dulci, was a lady of outstanding character, an honours graduate, she ran a holistic centre, treating people for all kinds of problems. I would have felt out of place, but there were some in the class who were, like me, ordinary mortals! Woodle, was a beautiful brown-haired woman, if one ignored the massive mahogany chip on her shoulder! She picked on everything and thought any criticism was aimed at her. It was obvious that she had 'issues' and would give us plenty of problems to solve, during our 'personal development' sessions. There was also a banker, teacher, psychology student, nurse (Me.), some unemployables and bored housewives.

First year was pretty basic stuff, probably because it was similar to the work I had done at the hospital and my own personal research into the subject. After the first year, having passed the exam, we were awarded associate membership of the college! Some left to set up in business, with this as their only qualification! Second year got serious, with essays on the pioneers of psychology, Sigmund Freud, (Sickman Fraud, to his friends.) Carl Gustav Jung was one of Freud's students. On leaving the group, in 1930, he went on to producing a valuable study of schizophrenia, was the originator of the concepts of introvert, extrovert and complex. His theory of archetypes and the 'collective unconscious, along with his philosophies helped to set him apart from all the rest. Karl Abraham, to whom much of the libido theory is due. Burrhus Fredric Skinner was a behaviourist who made many valuable contributions toward our understanding of cause and effect. There were dozens of others who made significant contributions, over the years, towards our understanding of the mind.

During the next two years I attended many, recommended, lectures and some that weren't. Analytic Psychotherapy in Chester, Neuro-linguistic Programming in Glasgow, Hypnosis in psychiatry at London, Ericksonian Therapy in Aberdeen, and so on and so on. The number of courses undertaken was proportional to your insecurity!

There was very little cohesion in the class, as we were such an insular bunch. A few dropped out, some left after gaining their second year certificate. The third year was taken up with relatively modern techniques; these included cognitive therapy, hypnotherapy and neuro-linguistic programming. This final technique is very effective when applied correctly and has seemingly unlimited applications. I struggled on to the end and gained my diploma! Now, I was deemed fit to practice as a hypnotherapist.

Nowadays, we are constantly bombarded by thousands of diet plans, weight-loss programs, healthy eating, fat people wanting to be thin people, but they are forced to eat chocolate, savouries, beef, etc? They are simply unable to resist eating those foods. This type of overeating, can be quickly wiped out! If you overeat on sweets, close your eyes and picture those sweets. Remember the times you were sick and bloated, all the problems you have experienced because of those sweets; skin rashes, loose bowels and the way people look at you when you are stuffing your face! See, feel and hear all these things. Describe the picture. Is it in colour? Black and white? Square or oblong? Now, open your eyes. That is called, the 'problem picture'. It is time to create, what we call, the 'desired outcome' picture.

This picture is how you see yourself, when you have achieved your desired weight loss. Again, close your eyes and make a picture of yourself, when you have achieved your goal and are the size that is right for you. Perhaps you will see yourself on the beach, looking great, or walking up the town, in your best gear. This is the picture of how you see yourself, when you have reached your goal! Everyone is looking at you, with admiration; they seem to know that you have done so well and are proud of you. Hear them cheering and clapping as you stride by, smart and elegant! Make this picture big and bright, warm and colourful.

Now, see the first, 'problem' picture, very quickly, smash this picture and replace it with the 'outcome' picture, then open your eyes. Do this, several times, faster each time. The 'problem' picture should be difficult to visualize, being replaced by the 'outcome' picture. This technique tends to wipe out the compulsion and allow you to ignore sweets. It is also effective on nail biting, smoking, etc.

Acute Blues.

My name was on the 'change of ward' list. I was being transferred, to the Admission ward. This was the busiest ward in the hospital, the nerve centre of the universe, the make or break factory! It was indeed fortunate, that I had accepted that my zenith had been reached, for, watching the ambitious staff, intelligent, efficient, knowledgeable and ingratiating made me cringe with envy. But I knew my limitations; well I thought I did!

It was difficult to keep abreast of all the procedures, examination trays, catheterisation tray, enema tray, spinal tap tray, etc, etc. They all had to be set out on a two-tier trolley, the 'clean' nurse worked of the top shelf, which was sterilised, the 'dirty' nurse used the bottom shelf to take away used instruments and bag the debris.

At the start of shift, I would draw up ten syringes of twenty millilitres Parentrovite, wrap the tourniquet round the patients' upper arm and inject the dark yellow fluid into his vein! These patients' were the alcoholics, and they needed the massive boost of vitamin 'B' to help prevent them going into the dreaded 'delirium tremens'. Because they were also dehydrated, fluids were essential, along with Phenobarbitone, for the shakes and Paraldehyde, a powerful sedative. For some it was too late! First the sweats then the paranoia, followed by seeing 'Lilliputians'; tiny beasties, 'pink elephants' 'snakes' 'spiders', even 'fairies' crawling all over their bodies. Sometimes they would go into 'status epilepticus', continuous seizures, Diazepam, would be given, per rectum, but if this failed to settle them, they would simply die of dehydration and exhaustion!

He was admitted, at midnight. It took eight men to carry the stretcher and put him onto the bed! One leg was hanging over the edge of the bed, but we were unable to lift it back onto the bed! This man was seven foot tall, built like a rhinoceros and, so we were informed, hated everyone and everything. When he walked into his local bar, everyone was so frightened of him they would buy him drinks all night! He was unconscious, but if he woke up, the staff unanimously decided that they would leave the ward! He never regained consciousness and died the next day!

The first year students were considered to be unable to think straight or logically. As they were there to be 'trained', the staff, were duty bound to help them overcome their handicap. "Would you please pop along to the female hospital ward and ask them for a Fallopian tube, we seem to have run out of them". The, eager to please, student would rush down the corridor, to the other end of the hospital and knock on the office door. The ward sister, on being asked for the item, would order the student to wait in the corridor while she looked in the store. The sister would return to her notes and after five minutes would inform the student that they had none in stock. "They may have them in ward 10, just across the corridor". Thanking her for her help the student would strut smartly to this ward and after five minutes, told the same thing. "Try the next ward along, they should have it". Six or seven wards later, the student would return to the ward and apologize for being unable to obtain the Fallopian tube. In the fullness of time, the student would learn, much to his embarrassment that this tube leads from the ovaries to the uterus in the female of the species! Other favourites, were Skyhooks, Gallivanting tubes, Long weights, the list was endless.

At about ten in the morning, the doctors would congregate in the ward office, with the charge nurse. Important details would be analysed; "I see Tweeters, had a skinfull last night. Made a frightful mess in the nurses' home. When are we going to get doctors who can hold their liqueur?" "Did anyone hear whatever happened to that 'robot' dancer chappie, nurse? The one that stole the drugs from the pharmacy!" A female doctor shows off her competence. "Yes, I read in the paper, he got sent down for six months, previous convictions and all that". They might then discuss the fact that the atmosphere on the moon was one fifth of earths, make suggestive remarks to the pretty, junior female doctors, who would smile provocatively and raise their skirts up to their suspenders! Eventually, they would, reluctantly, spill out onto the ward. The senior staff nurse would wheel the trolley, piled high with the patient's 'case notes', to the foot of each bed. The consultant responsible for each patient's care would flick through their notes, ask them how they were feeling, and then swish rapidly to the next bed. If a patient had a problem, heaven forbid, for the senior staff nurse had to quickly and succinctly 'fire it out'. In the event that the consultant ignored you, then you would try again, tomorrow!

"How are you today, George? Did you sleep well? Fine, we will see you again tomorrow". "Have you slept well, Harry? I see you still have that ocular contusion! Either cut out the fisticuffs or learn to duck!" "Good-day, Mr. Bandjii, you're doing very well. Things will soon clear up". (Alzheimer's?). Brave staff nurse dares to interrupt. "Mr. Bandjiis' pulse seems to be irregular sir, possibly cheyne-stokes, sir." The effort turned his face red as he caught his breath. "What the hell is going on here?" screamed the consultant. "When did a nurse become qualified to make diagnoses? It took me fifteen years to presume that I could offer an opinion as to a diagnosis". "Sorry, sir. It won't happen again, sir!" The red face turned purple, his breathing stopped. "I should bloody well think not! "You excuse for a nurse". Turning to the patient, "My assistant will check up on you, Mr. Bandjii, this very day. Possibly a touch of wind. Enjoy your lunch!"

Mr. Bandjii died, while eating his lunch! For months after, I would panic whenever I had a 'touch of wind?'

Although it was promotional suicide, I needed to get out of the ward. Certainly, there were many positive things happening there, but it was too cutthroat and fast for my feeble excuse for a brain! I was not happy! Asking for a transfer, to another ward, was a major inconvenience to the nursing officer, but, as another nurse had asked for a shift also, I was in luck! That is, if I could handle being locked up for twelve hours a day?

It was a warm, airless, boring evening. I decided to stroll up to the ward, to see if 'babe bait' wanted a game of cards and a blether. To get to his ward I had to cut through the female side. As I slipped in the side door, Lucie appeared like a dream. The silk blouse accentuated her femininity, as did the skin-tight jeans. Pressing her body gently against my back, I felt the cool points of her nipples, then the warmth of her generous breasts, her hands stoking my passions. An old female patient almost bumped into us in her haste to go out the door. My passion collapsed as I remembered our advice from the nursing school principal. 'It is an offence to use your position to gain favours from patients of the opposite sex. At all times you must exercise discretion and maintain a clinical and professional attitude. Any malpractice will be dealt with severely by legal proceedings and instant dismissal!'

'What if that had been a nursing officer!' 'All my work would have been for nothing!' I hurried down the long corridor; Lucie struggled to keep up. "Please don't leave me. We can go up by the pond, it's so peaceful and quiet there". In my mind, we were lying on the velvet grass; bodies locked in sensual ecstasy, her eager body urging me to greater heights of heart pounding, thrusting delights! To hell with it! Turning round, to whisk her up to the pond, I glimpsed her disappearing up a side corridor with a huge male patient! My evening lay in ruins, as was my battered passions. I returned to my room and had the most hellish nightmare, as I tossed and turned in my cold frigid bed!

There was lots of 'hanky-panky' goings on, between patients and patients, staff and staff also patients and staff! Because patients were away from home and staff were able to understand their illness and accept them openly, it was hardly surprising that they would be drawn to the staff. It was probably the first time that they had received any compassion and help. In addition to all this, they would be on medication that made them more relaxed and carefree! The result was a bubbling cauldron of emotional anarchy! The temptations were endless. This accounted for the high turnover of staff, who either ran off with a patient, were caught 'on the job', or were unable to face their demons! There was, inevitably, some staff that would take advantage! Although everyone had their suspicions, it was difficult to prove and even harder to prevent. One young and beautiful female would save all her cigarettes, stand at the back of the cafe and give one to anyone who would have sex with her! The queue was very long!

Staff could also be a problem! Nurses Tom and Tina's relationship hit the skids when his drinking escalated. He decided that she must be having an affair. Why else would she harp on at him to stop drinking? Tina bolted from the nurse's home, as Tom loaded cartridges into his over and under shotgun. Chasing after her, he almost has her in his sights, when the police intervened.

On the hospital grounds, the matron was enjoying a game of football between patients and staff. A junior doctor, who harboured a massive chip on his shoulder, convinced that matron was his archenemy. On spotting her across the field, he raced toward her, shouting and swearing. Matron ran round the field and would have been battered to a pulp, if four nurses had not restrained the doctor.

Locked Ward Lunacy.

It was like being in prison! Keys' jangling, doors slamming, locks clanging. I had arrived in ward 'F'; I could not imagine what the 'F' stood for! There were numerous nurses, to look after the forty or so patients. All of them had a bad reputation for violence, impulsiveness, perversity, dishonesty and possibly much more; and that was just the staff! However, this ward was run like a disciplinarian's dream.

When patients were admitted or transferred to this ward, were taken to the dormitory, stripped, bathed, and then dressed in pyjamas, dressing gown and slippers. They were then escorted through to the main ward, to await the visit from the duty doctor. This could take a couple of days! The general rule was, 'come in, sit down and shut up'. Once the doctor had assessed the patient, medication would be prescribed, given and hopefully accepted. The patient would then be interviewed by senior staff and, if deemed safe and cooperative, would be allowed to wear his own clothes.

In the morning, the patients were encouraged to get up, standing by their beds, they would be counted and then marched through to the main ward. The unruly youngsters, some as young as ten, were restricted to a corner of the ward. A junior and two nursing assistants would be allocated the impossible task of keeping them in order. Medicines were dished out, before breakfast; no one was allowed to refuse. New patients quickly learnt that a refusal was not permitted. In the event that they did refuse, they were restrained and the staff nurse held his nose while he poured the syrup into his mouth, which was then held shut until swallowed; basic, But it usually worked. On the rare occasions that this strategy failed, an injection of the medicine would be drawn up. Even if the patient then decided; he would take the syrup; he was given the injection, into the right upper quadrant of the buttock. They seldom repeated their mistake!

A full Scottish breakfast of a plate of porridge, then bacon, egg, sausage, black pudding and beans, washed down with a cup of strong tea. The ward toilet was locked, it was only opened after meals and then for twenty minutes, The exception was on a Wednesday! At 10 am, all the patients would be given a 20 ml. dose of laxative syrup! After thirty minutes and not before, the toilet door was opened to a stampede of defecators! The moans and groans of relief, was a constant source of amusement to the senior staff, who chose to have their tea break at this time. Some patients would have an 'accident', so, they had to be taken to the dormitory, bathed and changed, then returned to the ward.

The patient called 'Tinker' lay on a blanket on the floor. He was unable to walk, due to the amount of medicine required to stop him attacking anything and everything. One day he bit a consultant, the next day all his teeth were extracted!

Farmer Jack, was one of the old 'worthies'? He was a 'burnt out' paranoid schizophrenic that could not be rehoused anywhere else. Whenever a doctor would visit the ward, he would shout out, "Grass is green, sky is blue." In his mind, this proved, conclusively, that he was sane!

One of the charge nurses' Mr. Black, had been a physical training instructor, in the army. He was a big, powerful man. Strolling round the ward, he would quote his favourite poet, Robert Burns, he always attended and made eloquent speeches at the annual 'Burn's night. 'Poor wee timorous beastie, etc. Any patient with his feet up on one of the coffee tables, littered around the ward, would receive a frightful glare. If that didn't work, they would receive a derogatory lecture, whilst being dragged onto the floor. 'If you cannot sit on a chair properly, then you will sit on the floor'. For some strange reason, he decided to take me under his wing! He encouraged me to read up on all the patients, showed me all the ward routines, and went over all the medications and dressing. He then taught me when and how to order the ward stock, how to approach patients and which ones to be wary of and at regular intervals, would recite a poem of 'Burns'. It was inevitable that I would make mistakes. At these times, he would look disappointed and hurt, but would say nothing. On the rare occasions that I did something right, he would puff his chest out, smile and say, 'Well done, son'.

On the rare occasions that a patient would attempt to attack Mr. Black, it would be over before it began. In the event of a knife attack, an item of clothing, or whatever was to hand, would be thrown into the face of the attacker, the weapon removed and the patient held down, whilst an injection was drawn up and given. The patient would be reassured that his actions would not be held against him, as it was merely a symptom of his illness. If any particularly dangerous patient went berserk, it was best to approach him in threes. The nurse in the middle would hold up a mattress, as the other two would walk on either side. Pinning the patient between the wall and the mattress, the arms grabbed and he could then be pulled down onto the floor, on top of the mattress. With experience, it was possible to assess a patient's mental state. When distressed, a number of symptoms may be evident. Eyes staring or shifting from side to side, face red or even white, mouth tight or uttering obscenities, veins on the neck standing out, flexing of muscles and clenching of fists, constant pacing up and down the ward, anything that was unusual for that particular patient. Sometimes the nurse could approach the patient, check what the problem was and either talk him through it or offer medication to alleviate the problem. It was more difficult with the paranoid and the psychopathic patient. They took much longer to get to know, as they were usually more secretive and cunning. Only when engaged in conversation, might you elicit that they had a problem on their mind!

Drug addicts could be very unpredictable. There was no way to guess how they would react when they were drying out! One regular would run the length of the ward, before diving, head first, into the huge cast iron radiator! Another simply threw himself against the wall or door, often knocking it flat! The worst patient of all these, was the homicidal maniac! He generally came in from the police cells in handcuffs, having attacked a police officer. On admitting him to the ward, they would remove the handcuffs and leave. Then all hell would let loose. As he banged on the locked door, demanding to be, let out or he would kill someone, we would be phoning round the hospital to get extra staff. Sometimes the sight of ten nurses would help to calm them down, but sometimes it simply inflamed the situation. Even after a violent struggle, when hopefully, no one was injured, an injection given into the upper, outer quadrant of the buttock, it would still be necessary to pin him down on the bed as he could maintain his anger for hours! It may be that he needed to receive a second injection!

Most of the staff had cars to get to work. I peddled to work most days though sometimes one of the nurses on my shift would give me a lift. He preferred to give females a lift because on the floor of the passenger side, there was a discreetly placed mirror, which helped him look up between their legs! A nursing assistant owned a beautiful, shiny black two-litre RS injection car; such a thrill, to experience the sheer power of its acceleration that pushed you deep into the luxury seating. Parking it in the staff nurses' parking space was a big mistake! This space was at a window, so the nurse could keep an eye on his car. He was furious that anyone would dare to rob him of his very own private parking space. Something had to be done to correct this oversight! Later that day, to the nursing assistants' horror, he saw long scratches on the roof of his car and a multitude of bird droppings all over the paintwork. He never parked there again and wondered why it did not happen to any other car parked there? He was not to know that the staff nurse had scattered breadcrumbs over his car roof!

It was bathing day! The bath in the dormitory, was filled with warm, soapy water, six patients were marched through and the cleanest one got in first. One nurse would shampoo his hair whilst the other did his privates and feet. Then out the other side of the bath, to be dried and powdered by another nurse, who also checked their nails, whilst the 'next cleanest' stepped into the bath. Shirt, vest, underpants and socks were changed. Each bath took about thirty seconds! The water was then changed for the next group. When we finished all the patients, we were rewarded by our breakfast. This was a real treat, because there was always plenty of grub, and it was free!

It was inevitable that, on occasions, violence would erupt! 'Ecles' was a boiling cauldron of hate and homicidal paranoia. A powerful six-foot of muscle, he had been taken from his mothers home, by the police. He had decided that his mother was poisoning his food, so she had to die! We talked, many times, about the beautiful scenery of his west-country birthplace, joked and laughed at life in general. We were destined to spend many hours in pleasant, superficial conversation, with his deep booming voice and maniacal laughter. He would often talk of his wonderful, adorable mother. "I have given her a terrible time. I hope she can forgive me". Even after her death, no doubt hastened, by the many beatings, he spoke fondly of her.

The floor was due its weekly wash! All the patients were lined up on chairs, against the wall. Blood was everywhere, as 'Ecles' ran down the line, punching each one in the face! By the time we reached him, he was sitting comfortably, reading a newspaper. "What the hell, was that about?" I screamed at him. "They were all moaning, because they had to shift their seats. That, should stop them complaining!" He said, looking very pleased with himself. The mandatory dose of Chlorpromazine was administered, but it was having no effect on his behaviour! There were many more acts of violence; fighting, throwing televisions through windows or tossing beds against the wall. On rare occasions, he would earn ground parole. One day, he absconded into town, and tried to tear a policeman in half! Finally, he was considered dangerous enough to warrant being sent to a hospital, for the criminally insane!

Anora, was the happiest she had been for such a long time. The staff were so kind to her and didn't fuss about her eating, she ate a small amount and felt comfortable with herself. Of course, Babe

Bait, might have had something to do with her mood! He was so considerate and kind, such a lovely person.

It was time for the weekly weights to be done. Anora stepped gingerly onto the scales. "That's great." Shouted the nurse. "You've gained two pounds. Well done." As she walked back to her bed in an accelerating state of panic, terrified at the thought of becoming fat, she knew that she must lose the extra burden! Going to the toilet, she put her fingers down her throat and quietly regurgitated all the contents of her stomach. She knew that it was fine, when the clear fluids came and then the black bile! She would need to be more careful in future, eat only green salads, hide the rest of her food and tuck a hot water bottle under her skirt, when she had to be weighed!

Over the next few months, she needed all her ingenuity to keep her secret. She continued to see Babe Bait, but kept him at a distance. He must not worry about my losing weight, maybe talking to his nurse and he might tell the ward. It had happened before, in her last hospital. All the panic, nurses pestering her to eat, never left during a meal and for an hour after, in case she put it up again! The constant weighing and encouragement to eat and drink and pretend to enjoy it! The look of horror from her folks, because she had lost so much weight. She couldn't, she wouldn't go through that again.

"I'm sorry BB, but this rash from the medicine I'm on makes my body all sore whenever I am touched". "It's just that time of the month!" "I don't want you to catch this cold of mine!" She had to wear gloves, so that when they held hands he wouldn't notice her bony hands! It was late autumn, going on winter, so she could wear a heavy jumper without any suspicion; in actual fact, she had three heavy jumpers on and two thick skirts! Lots of make-up was needed to hide her, too white, skin and disguise the prominent cheekbones. She had to shave her face to get rid of the soft hairs that were there. At mealtimes, she would quickly swap her plate with the woman next to her, who would greedily gorge it down.

When she could no longer stand the look of anguish on BBs, face, she sent him a letter. 'My parents forbid me to have a relationship whilst I am in hospital. It will hopefully not be too long before we are both discharged and we can be together, always'.

When all the fat in the body has gone, the system starts to devour the muscles. As metabolism takes place, the poison that is produced, damages the kidneys and closes down the natural defences, ravishing the body! Usually she would be up and dressed before the nurses came round in the morning, but today it was impossible. She was paralysed, frozen and there was a loud banging in her head? The nurses were mortified when they realized the extent of her malnutrition. The duty doctor was called and she was transferred to the general hospital. Anora dreaded seeing her parents, staring down at her with that look of disappointment and self-pity. But, she did not need to worry about that, for despite the injections of antibiotics and vitamins, the tube pumping glucose into her, she lapsed into a coma! 'There is still some fat at my calves. Maybe I can get rid of that once I'm up again!'

A week later, Anora, passed away. An inquiry decided that nothing could have been done to save her, though lessons would be learnt from the tragic case!

A/C. D/C

"I'm getting married and I am worried about my sexuality". He seemed like a nice lad. Well dressed, clean and quite good looking. It was tempting to tell the joke. 'How do you recognize a homosexual on a housing estate? They always use the back passage! Or. Give us a kiss and I'll tell you! Sometimes jokes are good; to break the ice, but maybe on this occasion it would be a trifle insensitive.

He continued. "A couple of years ago, I was out for a drink with my mates. As I staggered home alone, through the village, at about two in the morning, I had to go to the toilet. I decided to have a pee over the side of the bridge. Suddenly, the headlights of a car blinded me and I turned round and told them to come and get some of the action. Unfortunately, it turned out to be a police car and I was charged with indecent behaviour. It even made the local paper. I was fined and put on probation". This was bad enough, but all his mates would crack jokes about queers. It made him wonder if he was normal. He had never done anything, 'queer', apart from that incident!

It was simply a case of reassuring him, that he was perfectly normal and he had just been unfortunate that the police had been there when he went to the toilet. The constant ribbing from his mates had compounded the incident, as had the publicity. If you are told often enough that you are stupid, bad, incompetent or queer, then it is inevitable that you will take it on board and behave as though you were stupid, bad, incompetent or queer. Einstein was told he was stupid, by his teachers, so he behaved stupid at school, but we all know how wrong they were! As Mark Twain once said, "I never let schooling interfere with my education!"

Old Timers

There were two dormitories with a sitting room sandwiched in between. At one end there was a store for all the sheets, pillowcases, blankets, pillows, rubber sheets, pyjamas, nightshirts and bed socks. The toilet was of to the right, behind the dormitory. It had a store for all the washing up materials, two baths, two wash-hand basins and a urinal. All the medicines were stored in the office, which sat at the back of the sitting room. Most of the patients remained in bed throughout the day; the others sat up in a chair all day, watching the television, except for two. One was a catatonic schizophrenic, who would carry out simple tasks; he was a huge, soft looking lump. He never spoke and always maintained the same empty expression on his face. You could lift his arm up and he would keep it there all day! The other was also a schizophrenic who was able to run messages and help with patient care. He was a young looking, thin, well-dressed man, who was always pleasant and smiling.

The ward was named, 'The Senile'. To some nurses, it was the punishment ward, where they went if they had committed some transgression, like being lazy or too many days off or they did not like your face! However, a few nurses actually enjoyed working in this type of ward? Tam the Bam, had been shifted down to the Senile after the charge nurse in his previous ward was unable to take anymore! The final straw came when Tam was asked to guard a Christmas tree, which was too high to stand up. "Make sure none of the patients fall over the tree. I'm going downstairs to get a saw and cut the tree down to size". On his return, Tam met him at the door, beaming from ear to ear. "It's ok, I've managed to cut the tree and it's standing up bonnie". The charge nurse was delighted; at last he had actually managed to do a job on his own. His face fell, as he looked at the tree. The top three feet had been cut off the tree!

He had a ruddy complexion, thick mop of brown hair; small round eyes topped by thin eyebrows, fat nose and a small mouth full of small grey teeth. He seemed not to have a neck, was squat with big hands and small feet. He had worked on his dad's farm after leaving school and for ten years, he worked crazy hours. He did everything on the farm, looking after the cattle and sheep, ploughing the fields, planting the seeds and never had a day's illness. His parents didn't seem the type to show any love or kindness, though he was comfortable and well fed. His father always' complained that he needed to do more work for less money. One day, Tam decided that there must be something better, so he walked the five miles to the hospital and asked to speak to the 'Chief'! Fortunately, he was speaking to Mr. Mortison, who thought he deserved a chance and arranged for him to move into the nurse's home. So, we were landed with the mammoth task of keeping him out of trouble!

Tam the bam, had been working in the Senile for three weeks; the staff nurse was going for a cup of tea. " Put some patients into bed Tam, I'll give you a hand when I get back". On his return, he was amazed to discover that the patients were in the wrong beds! "Why have you put the patients in the wrong bed?" Looking round at his handiwork, Tam scratched his scalp. "Well, they all look the same to me, friend".

The first job was to get the patients washed and shaved. The ones who were bed-ridden, would be done in their bed, the others were put onto a wheelchair, taken through to the toilet and washed, shaved and dressed there, then transferred onto their easy chair. The grumpy patient, called 'Twisty', was always reserved for the new nurse on the ward. While you were shaving him, he would suddenly lash out with his one good arm and strike you across the face. Then it was time to serve breakfast and most of them needed help to eat it. Then the beds were made and one of the charge nurses, 'Toad', would check they were made properly by dropping a penny on the middle of the bed, if it didn't bounce he bundled all the sheets to the middle of the bed and you had to start again! Toad was a particularly nasty piece of crap! Small and balding, always immaculate, always looking for a problem with his cruel, venomous eyes, strutting round the ward, like the 'poisonous dwarf' that he emulated so well. If he didn't like you, he made your life hell! You would be assigned all the dirtiest jobs, criticized mercilessly and sent for your breaks last. He took an instant dislike to me!

A few of the patients required their dressings to be changed. Usually the injuries were from bedsores or infections; sometimes it was due to self-injury! Because these patients were old, one was a hundred, it took a long time for wounds to heal and sometimes they would not heal and you just had to keep the wound clean. 'Mahogany', was the longest serving patient. His admission, at the age of eighteen, was with a diagnosis of, 'Dementia Praecox', which was the earlier name for schizophrenia, due to the illness developing before maturity! His name derived from the darkened skin, which was a side effect from his medication. Now, at the age of ninety, he remained in bed all the time, except when he went to the toilet, his bed was next to it. He never spoke and the only sound he made was a hearty laugh, probably in response to his 'voices'. Were they telling him a joke? He was perfectly healthy, but preferred to stay in his bed?

One of the duties, which some of the staff actually enjoyed, was 'evacuation day'. This meant that all the bed patients, unless they had diarrhoea or were dying, would be wheeled through to the toilet, placed on their left side on a cushioned board that was laid on top of the bath. One end of a rubber tube was inserted up their back passage. At the other end was a funnel, into which was poured a mixture of one-pint warm water to a walnut sized lump of soft soap. In the event that this failed to produce a copious amount of faecal excrement, then the dreaded, 'manual evacuation' would be executed!

The doctors would only visit if requested to do so, by the staff. They would also call at the ward to certify a death and transfer another patient into the empty bed! Losing a patient was a depressing business, but you had to move on or you couldn't do the job. It was unlikely that any of these patients would 'get better', so the best you could do was make them comfortable and content. The charge nurse on the other shift was called, 'The White Witch', this was because he was into water divining. Using a divining rod, he would go round the patients in bed and tell which ones were wet? He was, in fact, a great lad. He was the longest serving nurse in the hospital and had a wealth of experience, which no one in his or her right mind would question. He stood six feet and four inches and weighed twenty-two stone!

The constant criticism and, to my mind, unfair treatment by Toad, was getting me down. Should I ask him to give me a chance to show that I was a good nurse? Or would I be wiser to let the dust settle and perhaps he would pick on some other poor sod! "Stop standing about you idle lump. Being an ingrate is no excuse for laziness. Why do they keep sending me all the rubbish nurses?" Toad walked past me into the office, without breaking his step. I snapped! With my face bright red, I followed him into the office, put my hands round his throat and pinned him against the office window. "If you ever talk to me in that manner again, I will put you through this window!" I walked out of the office shaking and carried on with my work. It didn't mater if I got the sack; there was no way I could stay under the same roof as that 'pigs dwarf'! Any moment now, I expected to be told to report to the Matron's office and given my marching orders. Toad was off the next two days and when he returned the atmosphere was completely different? I was treated with respect, got off on the early breaks and he even smiled at me? Had it all been an initiation test? Does this mean I had passed?

Tam the Bam was obviously unhappy. His constant blunders and inability to adapt to ward routines meant he was constantly struggling to do his work and get any satisfaction from it. Perhaps he had made a mistake, leaving farming life! Why it had not occurred to anyone, was a mystery? Attached to the hospital, the cottage farm down the road, was used as a market garden. Patients were instructed on how to cultivate all kinds of vegetables and fruit. Would it not be wise to send Tam the Bam there and he would be in his element! He was pushed to apply and, sure enough, Tam was pleased as punch, working the land and showing the patients all the tricks of the trade.

There always had to be a problem! This one was called 'Darky Dan', a nursing assistant from the Caribbean. It wasn't that he was a bad lad; just that he had difficulty staying awake! Probably the fact that he drank rum all day, contributed to his condition! Often, he would be found, sleeping in a chair, with the patients and had to be constantly roused to do his work! One night, we were putting the patients to bed. On glancing back down the line of settled patients, there was Darky Dan getting the patients up! "What the hell are you doing, Darky, its night-time, we're putting them to bed!" His crumpled white coat and bleary eyes told us that he had just wakened from a sleep. "Now, now, whities, you mustn't take the piss, just because of my golden skin." It was only when he was shown the evening program on the television that he believed us.

Management had finally had enough, when Darky Dan made a phone call to his sister, who was a surgeon in Australia. This, in itself, was not a problem, but the fact that he was phoning from the matron's office, did nothing to endear him. On putting himself through to the front reception, Jinny asked for the number. "Put me through to the Sydney General hospital, immediately." A ruffled, indignant voice responded. "Who's this, on the phone? I can't authorize a long distance call." As matron entered her office, Darky responded. "You've got to put me through to Sydney, my sister's a surgeon there and she can get down here and get my brain sorted. It just isn't working anymore!"

Nightmare.

One of the duties allocated to the night superintendent, was a routine check round the nursing home. This was by way of a security check, making sure all the doors were locked and there was no hanky-panky going on! By a sheer fluke, as he passed the door of one of the first year male student nurses, he heard a dreadful gasping sound. Using his master key to get in, he found him hanging from a light fitting. He called himself 'T-bone'. Cutting him down, the 'night super' applied mouth-to-mouth resuscitation then shipped him up to the hospital ward. It was a week, before 'T-bone' finally broke down and, sobbing hysterically revealed all! However, this was one story that would be anyone's nightmare. The 'bush telegraph', was having a field day! Rumours, suppositions, suspicions and half-truths, were rolled into a believable tale.

Struggling male students were being offered extra tuition at night. After their lesson, they would be offered a 'nice cup of tea'. The problem was, they would wake up hours later, in their own bed, totally confused. This happened to 'T-bone', but the 'nice cup of tea' did not have the desired effect on him! Although extremely groggy, he was aware of being undressed, fondled and an uncomfortable bodily sensation, for the entire world, like constipation.

It was five days before the bleeding, from his back passage, finally cleared up. He doubted that it could be piles, as his doctor suggested. But, what else? The dreams at night were vivid, painful and always returned to the groggy experience that he had somehow reinvented. Surely, it must all have been in his imagination.

Realization was worse than his nightmares! Waking suddenly from his half-sleep, it struck him as so obvious, like a thunderbolt! At first, there was confusion, then disbelief, followed by sadness. Acceptance flooded in, like an overflowing, putrid sewer! Revulsion was followed by a sense of betrayal, which was converted into a rage against the world, then the one person responsible, himself! How had he managed to delude himself for so long? He was finally able to see himself for what he was a dirty, filthy nobody, who would always fail. That was when he decided to die!

'Sodium Amytal powder is stirred into the 'nice cup of tea'. It is so easy. Just wait until it takes effect, help them back to their room, undress the darling, a bit of 'rectal probing', then, by morning, everything would be forgotten!' His moist tongue flicked over his full lips and he brushed back a lock of black shiny hair, as he savoured these many, orgasmic moments! 'I'm actually doing the buggers a favour, they should be grateful to me for initiating them into these wonderful experiences, who else would even bother with them?' He ran his long fingers through his black, wavy hair and checked that he had enough capsules to concoct his next 'nice cup of tea'.

For some, unexplained reason, Sam the Sham, was never seen or heard of again. But, we all knew why. Didn't we?

Ho, Ho, Ho.

It was that time of year again! The ward decorations were dragged out of their hiding place and placed in neat piles, depending on where they were to be hung. There was a prize each year for the best-decorated ward. Most of the wards also had a party and patients from all the wards would be invited. A volunteer band or a disco usually supplied music. Tonight was our party night! The ward was a glittering mass of tinsel and coloured lights. Stacks of crisps, nuts, cakes, sandwiches, cans of lemonade were piled on the line of tables covered with gold and silver foil. On a separate table, hard against the wall, a huge tea urn was sitting beside the sausage rolls. It was almost time to begin and patients were starting to wander in with their nurse escort. Patients in wheelchairs were ceremoniously placed beside the food and drink.

Some of the patients in our ward could not stand the flashing lights and loud music, so we had given them a wee party earlier. Now they could go to bed and rest in peace. As I organised the other patients, sitting them down and giving them a drink of lemonade and a bag of crisps, Babe Bait walked in! He looked terrible, hair uncombed, unshaven, clothes all crumpled. "Can we talk? I barely heard him, as the band started tuning up. "I'm sorry, BB, I have to keep the boys in line. Come round in the morning, we can have a blether then". Without a word, he turned and left the ward.

The night passed without incident, apart from a patient from another ward trying to smuggle in a bottle of whisky! One had a major seizure and a female dancing naked! There was plenty of staff present; so all incidents were dealt with easily and quickly. We all took notes of when the other wards were having their parties and deciding which ones we should attend. When all the patients had gone back to their wards and ours were tucked up in bed, we formed a line at one end of the ward. Each nurse carried a black bag, which was filled with empty bottles, cans, bits of decorations, and empty crisp bags as we walked up the ward. The metal foil and tables were folded up and returned to the stockroom. The silence was awesome.

Next morning, I was on the early shift; we were informed that a male patient was missing and volunteers were asked to help in the search. After searching the hospital to no avail, checking that he had not just gone home, the police were called in and with the help of a sniffer dog the massive grounds were sectioned off, a group sent to each section and the hunt began! Most of them thought that he had just gone into town got pissed and was sleeping it of. He was found at the pond, lying on the bank, with his head in the water! He had been dead for twelve hours. It was Babe Bait!

Had he decided that he had suffered enough through his illness? Did a voice tell him to do it, or had he become depressed? The idea that he loved Anora so much that he chooses to join her was discounted, because his illness is reputed to blunt the emotions and the medicine would further tend to diminish responsiveness. Whatever the reason, he was gone and I missed him.

'You are a professional nurse and you cannot allow emotions to cloud your judgment or affect your conduct', matrons voice, stern and shrill, would continue, 'always maintain a clinical attitude with detached consideration and you will be a credit to your chosen profession'.

'Well, that's another one for the statistics' Ama Tird, cheerfully informed us; 'his bed will not be empty for long'.

'Life must go on', 'We come from ashes and return to ashes', 'No use crying over spilt milk', 'it will all seem better in the morning'. These phrases seared through my consciousness then disrupted my thoughts, causing confusion and numbness. Shouting a cheerful goodnight to the patients and staff, I strode down to my room. As I opened the door my emotions took over and I cried. I was not a 'credit to the profession'.

At one time in my life, I was standing on the swing bridge at the canal locks, looking down at the swirling, black, welcoming water. It was two in the morning; I had just finished an ambulance trip to Ullapool and was making my way home. Many things were getting me down; we never seemed to have enough money, even though I worked every hour God sent. I would faithfully hand over all my wages and only took enough money for my meagre supply of rolling tobacco. Often the charge nurse would give me cigarettes that were spare from the ward stock. My mood had suddenly collapsed. Everything in my tiny world caved in, like a deck of cards. I had nothing, was nothing and tomorrow was just a black hole.

The black, syrupy water looked so inviting. The powerful current would suck me down, pressurising me into unconsciousness and I would be serenely ushered into the carefree oblivion of utopia! It was hypnotically drawing and seemed the perfect answer as I felt myself leaning over and about to topple in.

Then it struck me, like a twenty thousand foot freefall with no parachute. All my problems stemmed from my inferiority and fears, that infected every area of my life, like a voracious cancer. But what if I took the 'bull by the horns' and decided to simply get on with my life, ignore these stupid ideas, enjoy the excitement and opportunities of tomorrow! At this moment it seemed inevitable that life could only change for the better. Anyway, if nothing changed, there was always the option of 'plan B', jump! Nothing in this world can even come close to the drastic step of taking your own life, so from now on life was a ball, by comparison. My rainbow had shone, helping me to regain hope.

The majority of suicides occur in the early hours of the morning. If a person is very depressed, it is unlikely they will be motivated to kill themselves. The crucial time is when they start to come out of the depression and gain that motivation to end it all. Perhaps they are afraid that the depression may return and they would rather be dead than face the torment again. It is estimated that twenty-percent female and ten- percent males, of the adult population have suffered a major depressive episode!

NIGHMARE FLASH.

Footsteps on the stair, here we go again. I would imagine that I was looking down from the ceiling, seeing myself, far below, as a rag doll. It was the only escape!

It was years ago when it first happened; Was I five or five and a half? Dad was great; we did so much together as a family. Mum was so happy. At six months pregnant, she was radiant and blooming. We would all enjoy walks along the seaside, through the woods and laugh at everything. He was full of mischief, such a handsome, kindly dad.

Then mum had to go into hospital, her tummy was sore, I heard someone mutter, 'could be a miscarriage!' That night, dad put me to bed, as I slipped between the cool, silky sheets; he started to cry in a hysterical fashion? His warm body was beside me, I felt his huge erection nudging against me. It was so nice to be kissed and cuddled. I sensed the urgency, as he roughly pushed my legs apart, ignoring my cries he rammed into me, the pain was mind numbing, my whole body erupted. I felt him shiver as he gave a loud howl. He smiled at me, the way he did when we played. His face clouded and he leapt out of bed, fumbling with his shirt and trousers. 'I'm sorry, I'm sorry, please forgive me; it's your mothers fault for not being here'. He was still crying as he tucked me in and kissed me goodnight. I thought I was going to die, my whole body screamed with the fire. What had I done wrong? Why did I have to suffer all this pain? I must be a bad daughter!

It happened again, a few nights later! 'Don't ever talk about this to anyone, not even your mother. It is our special secret' I couldn't stop sobbing, I was very confused, hurt, frightened and yet, strangely happy? Was I special? Was I wrong to feel all these funny emotions that I didn't even understand? My 'special' treatment continued every second or third night, until mommy came home, two weeks later.

Mum was home and everything was happily 'normal' again. That is, if you ignored the worried looks dad would give me, behind mum's back! I started sleepwalking; mum would put me back to bed. It wasn't long before he came to me, in the middle of the night, 'It's alright, your mums sound asleep, just don't make a sound'. He hurriedly pushed my legs apart, kissing and cuddling me he gently pushed into me, but the pain was just as terrible. At times I would let out a yelp, 'Don't be bad', he would snap, 'you mustn't waken your mum, she needs her sleep'.

Our lovemaking, became a regular, two or three weekly event. Sometimes I would notice my mum looking at me strangely; did she know what was going on under her nose, and if she did, why did she not do anything? Questions ricocheted round my brain, chest, stomach and heart. What was happening? Why did I feel so terrible about it? When would it stop? Was it supposed to happen? Dad said, 'It's because I love you and you need to be taught'. Then he would kiss me and put his finger to his lips, 'not a word now'.

As time passed I began to suffer all kinds of sickness; loose bowels, breathing difficulties, skin rashes, unable to eat, then when I did eat I was sick as a dog. My moods would swing rapidly from high to low for no reason and when my periods started, I would bleed constantly! Dad started buying me presents and giving me money. Later in life, I would realise that he was treating his daughter like a whore!

My sister came home and my father ignored me for a couple of months. She got all the attention. Had I done something bad? 'Say hello, to your beautiful, baby sister'. Was I not beautiful too? Her big blue eyes, soft curly hair and supersoft skin. I hated her! Then I would feel guilty, but why should I? At times I would really love her, I could not do enough for her; washing her, dressing her, then taking her for long walks.

Then, one night, dad came back to me, I felt happy that I was getting attention again.

At the 'old' age of sixteen, I convinced my folks to allow me to stay at my aunties. She had more space, I needed a quiet place to study, for my highers and, though I could never say, it was starting to get me down, being used by my father! Years later, I began to wonder if dad was interfering with my sister! She was starting to suffer the same symptoms as I had. Surely, he wouldn't have sex with our lovely, delicate sister?? It was incomprehensible!

It was only after I had help, myself, that I was able to broach the subject of abuse with my sister. She eventually broke down, after I told of my experiences. "Yes, he does have sex with me, but he says it is only because I am so beautiful and special. I can't say anything, because dad says it is my fault for being so provocative".

It took years of embarrassment and heartache, to get him charged, he even served a couple of years in prison. Mum never spoke to us again, said we had made it all up. How could she be so blind, toward her monster of a husband?

One Session Cure

"Hello, I'm phoning to ask if you can give my daughter a session for her nervous problem. It's by way of a Christmas present." After gleaning more specific information, I accepted the challenge! Sonia was nineteen years old, plain though attractive and was a manageress in a shoe shop. She had a boyfriend and an ex, who could not handle being dethroned! Presenting problem was her great difficulty getting to work. This was because she could not bear to stand on a crack! This meant that she had to walk miles to avoid any cracked surfaces. She couldn't go out at night for fear of standing on a crack in the dark.

Usually there is a cycle of similar behaviour, dating from childhood. Sure enough, it transpired that in school she had a compulsion to touch walls! To get from one class to the next, she had to walk round by the wall, touching it as she went! There were other short episodes of compulsive behaviour and she was able to tie these in with periods of stress; examination times, start of her menstruation, etc. Sonia reluctantly informed me that her boyfriend and her ex, were both violent toward her, but she was too embarrassed to tell her family or friends. I always get very angry, when violence is perpetrated on a weaker individual. It was difficult for me to hide this emotion!

Since she now understood the link between her compulsions and stress, it should be easier to guide her toward a resolution of the problem. "I want you to realize that you have walked over hundreds of cracks when you came up the stair". She squirmed uncomfortably, taking in the information. "Under the carpet the wooden steps have splits in the planks; also, if you look at an apparently smooth pavement with a magnifying glass, you will notice a network of cracks". I had already established that her main submodality, or how she perceived her environment, was mainly visual as she stressed how things appeared to her. I decided to use a rapid flooding technique and throw in reciprocal inhibition, for good measure!

Close your eyes and count down from ten to one, breathing out and letting go more with each count. Now imagine you are at the top of the stair with all the cracks. When I say 'now', see yourself walking backwards, rapidly, down the stair. When you reach the bottom, open your eyes". "We will do this several times, each time faster". Each time she opened her eyes, I asked her a simple question, like, 'what paper do you read?' 'What is the day after tomorrow?' Afterwards, I asked her how she felt about her past fears of walking on cracks! "That's odd, I feel silly now, that I had even thought about something as unimportant as cracks!" She had obviously lost her obsession, for she spoke about it casually. Her body language was also relaxed. "Your behaviour was not silly at all; in fact it was helping you deal with your stress. How about using a more acceptable behaviour, like jogging, or rock climbing!" "No, that is just not me!" She pondered for a moment. "My stress at the moment is caused by the nasty behaviour of my boyfriends! If I give them their marching orders, then I can start taking control of my life". As she left the house, I watched her from the window, walking over the cracks without a thought!

Obsessive-compulsive disorder, can affect every facet of our lives. The automatic need to touch the walls as we pass by them. The gnawing doubt, 'did I turn the gas off'? 'Maybe I forgot to switch off the lights before coming to bed'? Ever had a problem, getting a catchy song out of your head? These can all be indications of a tendency toward obsessive-compulsive disorder and if you get stressed they could explode into a problem.

Obsessions are recurrent, persistent ideas, thoughts, images or impulses that are ego-dystonic, e.g. outside our control. They involve thoughts that don't make sense or are extremely distasteful. A heightening of agitation and anxiety can be experienced if we attempt to ignore or suppress them. Compulsions are repetitive and seemingly purposeful behaviours, performed according to certain rules or in a stereotyped fashion. Although it provides a release of tension, the senselessness of the behaviour is recognized and no pleasure is derived. Depression and anxiety are commonly associated with this. Often there is phobic avoidance of situations around the obsessive content, such as dirt or contamination.

Two Worlds Collide.

The tranquillity of the all male, locked ward was to disappear forever! It had been decided to redesign the ward to have a mixed sex intensive therapy ward. Apart from the charge nurses, all the staff had to re-apply for the positions in the new ward! Patients and staff were all shipped out to another ward, while the old ward was made habitable for both male and female patients. The dormitory was split into two sides, fifteen males and five females. This was a big reduction in numbers, though there were to be an increase in staffing levels. As an added bonus, we were going to be working with female nurses!

For the few months, while the new ward was been constructed, we struggled on in our make-do ward. Most days we would have to go round to the old ward door, to collect a patient who was banging at the door to get back to his old haunts! The patients would wander round the ward, confused and unsettled, trying to make sense of their new surroundings. All the staff made regular sorties, to check on progress and collect things left in the ward. It was difficult to keep the ward running, as though everything was normal, because everyone was on edge wondering what would be our fate. Perhaps we were all going to be shifted to other wards, using the new ward as an excuse to get the team broken up!

I applied for this wonderful new, Intensive therapy, short stay, mixed sex unit. An informal interview was arranged and, with much trepidation, I marched into the interrogation room. You never knew when or where he would strike; small beady eyes topped a thin supple torso. The Snake was a nursing officer famed for his deviousness and apparent lack of any human emotion. "Tell me why we should employ you in this new ward? How do you think you would be an asset there?" Did his lips move? "My contribution, apart from my locked ward experience, would hopefully be in the running of group therapies. These would include general supportive groups, to enhance cohesion, self esteem, relaxation and more specific groups to address aggression, delusional beliefs and self perception". The Snake listened intently, trying, no doubt, to find a hole in my ideas. I tried to outstare him, but, as he never blinked or looked away, I had to give up and accept that I was only human after all. "I'll get back to you, later this morning. Thank you for your time". He slithered off, probably to find someone who would explain, in nonprofessional terms, what I had been talking about. It was time for my second interview; he invited me into his own office. It was like a tropical rain forest, hot and moist. Only the lamp, shinning in my eyes, was missing. The morning interrogation was under way! "You spoke about running groups in the new ward, what type of dynamics might one expect from these meetings?" Every 's' was an excuse to hiss and spit. Pretending to blow my nose, I wiped off the specks of saliva. "Usually, the clients would experience a set of reactions within the group. These would include, pairing, modelling, revelations, denial, reflections, silences, scapegoating and hopefully insights and resolution of some of their problems. Usually their behaviour is automatic; they do things without thinking about the consequences, in groups we can examine their actions and give them more acceptable ways to behave". He scribbled something on his folder. "It would seem that you have a working knowledge of the subject, so I will recommend that you be selected to join the team, providing you can supply a record of the groups activities and, hopefully, progress!" A scaly hand shook mine; I thanked him, went back to my room, washed my hands and changed my sweaty shirt!

The beds and lockers were set out, dictated by the plastic curtain rails, from which hung the, too plain, nylon curtains. In the past we could view all the patients in the ward, from our office, but we wondered how we could know what was going on behind the curtains? To our amazement, they had laid a grey speckled carpet over the wooden floor. We knew it would be destroyed as soon as the patients stubbed out their cigarettes on it! The office was situated between the male and female dormitories. Behind the office lay the single secure bedroom, with the bed bolted to the floor, reinforced door and window with unbreakable glass. A female toilet had been built off the entrance corridor to the left of the outside door. Even the ward had been blessed by a carpet, new chairs, new television and even a new office! In the corner of the dinning room we had a bench-press installed? The male toilets had been divided to add on a female ablution! In the new clinic room, beside the ward kitchen, hours were spent stocking up the cupboards and shelves with all the medical supplies; syringes, needles, swabs, intravenous and intramuscular ampoules of antipsychotic, anticonvulsant, antidepressive, antispasmodic and all kinds of other anti-drugs! There were bandages, plasters, creams and lotions, examination trays, etc, etc, etc. At last we were ready to open the new ward!

The ward policy was to accept patients for only a short stay, then return them to their ward or onto a rehabilitation unit. Inevitably we had long stay patients because no other ward could take them. These patients were violent, unpredictable or just immoveable. At first it was great; we only had six male patients and six staff per shift! This gave us the opportunity to acquaint ourselves with the ward and everything in it. Frequent ward meetings, to go over the ward policy, flexing our muscles on the bench-press machine and elbow wrestling, drinking tea and coffee and even nursing our patients. There was an awful hush when the phone rang and we knew our halcyon days were over!

We should have guessed that our first female patient would be deadly Deirdre! Her learning difficulties, violent temper and nicotine cravings, made her a virtual time bomb. "Please give us a ciggy. I'll give you one back as soon as I get my money!" The old woman looked her in the eye. "You didn't pay back the last two. I can't afford to keep you in fags!" Deirdre leapt of her chair and slapped the old woman very hard. "You're nothing but a fucking cunt. You're just jealous because all the men fancy me!" As she drew her hand back to strike the cowering woman again, a nurse pulled her back and received a slap for her troubles. Two male nurses escorted her to the Intensive Therapy Mixed Sex Secure Ward, or for short 'Lock-up'!

Fifteen stone of mean fat, her black hair framed an ugly, flabby face. Her smile exposed black teeth and foul breath. "Nice to see you again. Where have you been? Got a ciggy for me, love?" I took a step back, before she could kiss me. "I'll have a look later. Have a seat there and tell me what happened". It was important not to say no to her and to divert her mind onto something else, anything else! We would just keep her overnight, tell her to behave herself and advise the staff to realize when she was going off, so they could divert the situation. Using our ward as a punishment was not to be encouraged, although it was inevitable. Gradually the ward filled up, but we had to keep a spare male and female bed in case of an emergency admission!

The staff all got on great. Probably because we knew we had to rely on each other to work together and watch our backs! In every ward you get the 'office boy'. This nurse will never be very far from the telephone. Most of the day he will be employed in office duties; filing, writing care plans, tidying up case notes, checking the off-duty or simply clearing the desk! Whenever the phone rang, he was the first there! In one way we were lucky, our 'office boy' was smart, and really helped to keep us all informed about the clerical side of things. Other staff preferred to arrange the ward supplies, making sure all the necessary stock was available and in the correct cupboard. Some times they would take a patient to help fold away the laundry or tidy up the bathroom. It could be quite therapeutic, folding shirts and trousers, stacking sheets and pillowcases, but I preferred to chat to the punters. It could be fascinating to hear all their stories and how they perceived their problems. If they were reluctant to talk, I used to make up my own version of what I thought their problem might be! If it was rubbish, then they would get annoyed and tell me where I was wrong and if I was close, they would carry on where I left off. In the event that a patient was too depressed or disturbed to speak, I would sit opposite them and mimic their posture, move as they moved and even breath in time to them. If this is done discretely it usually helps to form a bond between the pair of you and can eventually lead to the person talking to you. If the person is very upset or angry it is best to keep your distance, but remain available!

Orchid's parents dropped her of at the ward and accompanied the consultant psychiatrist to his office. She sat on a chair, taking in all her new surroundings. This creature was, from head to toe, perfection! Tall, with lily-white skin, waist length, honey-blonde hair, long slender neck seemed to draw your eyes down to her small, prominent breasts, flat muscular stomach, narrow hips, long strong legs and tiny feet. I could imagine her modelling for the figures depicted on a Grecian urn!

"Would you come into the office, please, so that I can take some admission details?" Without a word, she followed me into the office. Standing beside me, she cradled my hand in hers; a shiver ran down my spine, as she stared intently at my fingers. Her voice was so sweet and yet, earthy! "Do you masturbate often?" My jaw dropped and my face flushed. "Only a joke! I'm sorry if I embarrassed you". Her smile wasn't a smile and I couldn't think why? Answering all my questions succinctly, in her earthy, sweet voice, she only hesitated when I asked her what she believed was the reason for her admission! "I have no idea. Perhaps the doctor will enlighten me!" Her dark blue eyes caressed my thoughts.

Her parents returned and spoke to her, then left the ward. For the remainder of the shift she sat alone at a coffee table, throwing dice and looking through a small book each time. She picked at her meal and drank some milk. The medical and psychiatric notes were ordered from the records office, but these usually took a couple of days to be delivered.

'Another day, another dime!' Sometimes that's all that seemed to mater. The ward was quiet and settled, patients and staff going about their business; filing this, writing that, checking the bins for tabbies, scraping out the tobacco and rolling a thin line into a piece of newspaper. We tried to discourage this practice, but some of the older patients preferred to resist progress?

Out of the blue Orchid got out of her chair, casually strode over to Deirdre and punched her on the chin! She then gracefully returned to her chair, picked up her dice and continued to roll them, each time checking her small book. "Why did you do that?" A shocked nurse, Angel asked her. "If you don't know, then you have no right to ask!" Angel tried to conceal her perplexed look and changed her approach. "What is that game you seem so fascinated with?" Orchid frowned and looked up at her. Angel stepped back, expecting an attack. The other staff sensed the tension. "It's not a game, you moron, it's a way of life! 'I Ching' has all the answers. It's an ancient Chinese manual of divination, based on eight symbolic trigrams and sixty-four hexagrams. The principle is based on, 'Yin and Yang', which is Chinese for feminine and male genitals!" Angel failed to hide her look of perplexity! "You must not attack people. Come and speak to the staff, before you do anything". She might as well have talked to the cat, for all the good it did!

The notes finally arrived, and as usual we had not been told the whole truth; it seemed to be medical policy to reveal only the nice information, and gloss over the unpleasant details. 'We just need to get his medication stabilized, then he can go home'. This usually meant that the patient refused all medication and we would go through the process of offering oral medication, then, when refused, getting him certified under the mental health act before we could give him an injection of an antipsychotic. A least four staff would be required to hold him down while receiving the injection and until he calmed down. It was a fine art, knowing when it was safe to release the patient. Sometimes you would release your grip on his sleeve and he would lash out at you!

Orchid's notes revealed that, physically she was in excellent health, but her behaviour over the last six months had gone from bad to worse; increasingly she would remain in her bedroom, at times refusing to come down for her meals. The music would be loud, and then there would be complete silence, all the time engrossed in her, 'I Ching'! Suddenly leaving the house with no explanation, she would do something totally unpredictable; break a window, swim in the river fully clothed or return with a male friend. The list was endless. Something had to be done as she was becoming more prone to acts of violence! We had been told about her unpredictable behaviour, but nothing of the violence. An emergency certificate was placed on Orchid to get her into hospital, all we had to do now was to observe and note her mental state so that the doctors could warrant a further, longer period in hospital. This would allow time to decide what medication might change her behaviour for the better. Only short-acting medication could be prescribed, when a patient was on an emergency certificate. After three days, if necessary, a longer intermediary certificate, lasting a month, could be applied for, through the courts. If deemed needful to detain a patient longer, then a further application is put through the courts and, of course, the patient can appeal against the section, through their solicitor. Patients are categorized as informal, which is a voluntary admission, or formal, if placed on a section of the mental health act, or detained, if they are admitted via the courts, under the secretary of state. These are referred to as, the criminally insane! There were also patients admitted through 'Social Work' orders and this was usually under very 'woolly' conditions, as everything had to be sanctioned through the patients social worker.

It was obvious that Orchid was a danger to herself and others, which was a sufficient criterion for her long-term detention in hospital. Although various medications were administered, her behaviour became more unpredictable and increased in violence. On visiting another ward, she viciously assaulted the staff nurse there. One morning she had been caught pocketing her tablets and it was discovered that there were many more lying in her locker! A depot injection, which is a slow release form of antipsychotic, was prescribed by her doctor and given in the upper outer quadrant of her right buttock! Orchid was then informed, that because she had difficultly taking tablets, she would receive an injection once a week. It was the first time that her pretty face portrayed the emotion she was feeling, 'horror'!

Pacing up and down the ward, she looked like all the other long term, demented patients, who matched her steps. Her face fluctuated, as she seemed to experience all her mixed-up emotions. Finally, she sat down on her chair and cast her dice, then referred to the 'I Ching' manual. After dinner, we were tidying up the tables, when Orchid calmly strode up to nurse Angel with her hand outstretched? Angel looked up, expecting her to speak and saw blood running down her left cheek! Looking down, to the outstretched hand, she saw a white ball with a strand dangling from it. This strand was the optic nerve! Orchid had pulled her left eyeball out of its socket!

The black eye patch, over the left eye socket, was very distinctive and made Orchid stand out in a crowd, she seemed very pleased with herself. After the 'incident' she was even more agitated. This meant that she had to be 'specialed', which meant that two nurses had to with her all the time. To make matters worse, it was obvious that Orchid was determined to pull out her other eye! The doctor was informed that it was only a matter of time before she damaged her remaining eye. The consultant psychiatrist was called and it was finally decided! Orchid was given powerful sedatives and rendered unconscious for several days, then reassessed! On coming round, she seemed more settled, but the problém now was her increased homicidal tendencies. After a number of serious assaults, there was no other option but to transfer her to the 'State Hospital'!

The group therapies were going well. Initially, I approached each of the six most violent patients and informed them that they had been selected as suitable candidates to participate in a special group experience as I felt they would be helpful to other members and we would also address their particular problem. They were also informed that there would never be more than six members and they would have their say on the running of the group. At the first meeting they were reintroduced to each other, this was a bit of fun, because most of them had been around for years. It was empathized that anything discussed in the group must remain secret; none of them could talk about it outside the group even among themselves. All material should be brought to the next group for discussion. We met twice a week for forty minutes.

At the start of each meeting I did a rapid form of relaxation, lasting five to ten minutes. This helped to settle the bunch and get them into the right mood. Each member was then asked how he or she felt at this moment and from this information came the basis for further discussion. The fact that most of them reacted to most situations with violence or aggression of some sort, was talked about and examined, strangely enough they enjoyed this, as it was a new experience. "Why do we react in this way?" "What would be a better way to react?" "How would things change and what would it achieve?" Usually they veered off at a tangent, but careful wording helped bring them back on track. Sometimes the members would decide a subject to discuss and this could be quite productive. Even members, who seldom contributed, were obviously helped through merely listening, as there was an improvement in their behaviour.

He was unkindly named 'Mr. Pipe Fitter'. This was partly due to his skill as a plumber; anything to do with plumbing systems was second nature to him. Even though only in his late twenties, he was in charge of a large team of plumbers. Gradually things worsened. At work, he would suddenly begin to throw things around as the workmen ran for cover. Afterwards they would ask him what was wrong, with a confused look at the mess around him, he would tell them to clean it up. Beating up his pretty wife was the next step, his excuse being, that the food had a queer taste! Clothes and money was missing! She was flirting with the man next door!

One morning on waking he was amazed to find his wife weeping and trembling. The room was totally destroyed. What had happened? Who had done this awful thing? What the hell is going on in this madhouse? Between sobs, his wife gave him the answer. "We were talking about a holiday, your face went blank and you stared right through me. Suddenly, you started throwing the furniture at the wall. After a couple of minutes you fell down, shaking and squirming on the floor for what seemed like ages then you just fell asleep. The doctor is on his way."

Totally bemused by the revelation, he was admitted to the ward for observation. Jet-black hair, dark brown eyes that peered intelligently over a roman nose, the sinewy, muscular body all pointed to a healthy individual. It was difficult to imagine that this pleasant, chatty lad was ill! Over the next few days it was realized that he was suffering from 'temporal lobe' epilepsy! The pre-epileptic state turned Pipe Fitter into a homicidal maniac! Minutes later he would suffer a major convulsive seizure, resulting in total amnesia for the whole episode. There was a great variety of bizarre behaviour, from stripping all his clothes off, making love to the pillar in the dormitory or shouting obscenities at the light bulbs! Sometimes he would attack patients or staff, but if we were lucky, someone would notice his blank stare and he could be removed to a side room where the whole thing could be controlled.

The seizures were reduced, by identifying 'triggers' that could bring on a fit. These included, stressful situations, bright, flashing lights and drinking too much fluid. Getting him to talk about how he was feeling and ways to resolve any bad feelings also helped. Anticonvulsive medication, such as Phenobarbital, Epanutin, Diazepam and Tegretol, were all tried and monitored to find the ideal combination. Slowly, but surely, his violence and convulsions were brought under control and he was given his first overnight pass! It was a disaster! He took the wrong bus and was found wandering round the countryside, totally confused and lost.

For a time he seemed so much better, with no problems, going home on pass and making plans for the future. This lasted only weeks, then the bubble burst! He went into status epilepticus, which meant him suffering continuous seizures, one after the other. Diazepam was given per rectum, fluids by intravenous infusion and he was transferred to intensive care. Unimpressed, despite all our efforts, Pipe Fitter passed away without gaining consciousness.

The condition is fairly common and has a long and distinguished clientele, which includes Byron, Van Gogh and Julius Caesar. The major seizures are the tonic-clonic seizures, involving periods of unconsciousness, which are called Grand Mal. Minor seizures are named Petit Mal and Jacobsonian, which do not result in unconsciousness, though can be accompanied by altered states of consciousness. These have been famously used as a defence in some criminal cases!

Kangaroo Court

Flaming red hair, with an attitude to match, she was dragged in by two social workers, direct from the court. 'Get your hands of me, you scabby lesbians'. The neutral stares from the social workers, told us they had seen and heard it all before. One actually spoke to us. 'As explained in my phone call, 'Phosfer' has been ordered here by the court under a 'place of safety' order. These are the necessary papers, along with a brief case history', placing them on the office desk she produced a form, 'sign this and we will be on our way'. Phosfer looked round the ward with her sparkling, green eyes, 'You didn't tell me you were taking me to a nuthouse'! The social worker, who seemed to be in charge, spoke, without looking at her, 'Don't be disrespectful, you will be perfectly safe here'. Handing her over to a couple of female nurses, they sped out the door, wishing us 'all the best', no doubt dashing off to save some other poor wretch!

Taking her into the dormitory, the female staff helped her remove her manly clothes. The denim jacket, shirt and jeans were filthy, as was her matted hair. A bath and a change of clothes made her appear slightly more feminine. She had recently become distressed and had been attempting to kill herself by throwing herself in front of cars, setting the house on fire and finally tried to hang herself, fortunately her husband found her and cut her down. The weeping, jagged line round her throat was evidence of her last failed attempt!

With increasing abhorrence, we perused her case-notes. Being an orphan, she had been raised in a small orphanage, ran by a couple, north of Australia, N.S.W. There were five girls and a couple of boys, all under twelve. The man and wife would take turns to sit with them at night, in the tiny dormitory. It transpired, that when the man was in charge, at night, he would construct a makeshift tent in the corner of the dormitory, where he could smoke and drink. He offered to share his cigarettes and drink with them, telling them how much he adored them. But, then he withheld the 'treats', saying they should be more grateful for his kindness, perhaps they could give him a 'treat' in return! Each child would be invited, in turn, to his tent, where he would make them perform increasingly vile acts of bestiality! Being a sadistic pig, meant his demands became more and more violent and sickening. Phosfer was amazed that she could accommodate his enormous penis, especially when erect! The fire that cut through her, was mixed with the feeling of excitement and a sense of being needed and loved? For many days after his rampage, the girls would bleed profusely. When his wife wondered why, he would explain, 'They must be having their periods!' His massive frame towering over her, daring a contradiction.

For a time, after leaving school, she coped well. She worked hard and developed her artistic talents. Her unusual scenic oil paintings demonstrated clever overtones of modernistic representations and sold well. After she married, they decided to come to Scotland. Two children followed in quick succession, then for no apparent reason her whole world imploded! Everything was a problem; it seemed that nothing would ever be right for a person so wicked and contemptuous like her! So determined was she, to kill herself, it was necessary to watch her day and night and even search her in case she picked up anything that she could use to harm herself. A can of juice ripped in half, gives you a razor sharp edge, cigarette lighters left lying around on a table, could easily be pocketed.

The most difficult time was when phosfer got her escorted parole to the recreation hall. As a squad of patients from another ward came into the hall, she would use them as a shield and slip out the door. Running along the corridor, she would make for the side door that led to the grounds. It became a routine for the staff at the hall to bleep the ward twice, from their radio, and a nurse from the ward would run to the side door. On seeing the nurse in her path, she would stroll back to the hall. Despite her continued determination to end her life, Phosfer coped well with hospital life and was even able to talk to some of the patients and, when necessary, a member of staff! Her primary nurse would sit with her, at the opposite side of the round table, for a half hour chat each day and it was noted that Phosfer, always smoking a fag, would appear distracted at these times! At one such chat, the nurse realised that it was more than smoke she was smelling. Quickly, looking under the table she saw the reason for the odd smell! Phosfer was holding the cigarette end against the skin on her forearm. On lifting up the long sleeve of her blouse, she revealed an arm that was black, up to the elbow. The skin on both arms, were charred to a crisp, due to the hundreds of times she had stubbed her cigarette on her arm. It was like looking at the black scales of a lizard!

As usual, I was working too many shifts to maintain an alert wakefulness. Letting the patients out the main door, so that they could attend their various therapies, I returned to the office to catch up with my notes on care plans and reappraisals, that I had agreed with my patients. It was the monthly assessment, to see if there had been any improvement in their condition. A finding of better or worse, was seldom the case, usually it was, 'no change'!

A shrill screech, made me jump. 'Has anyone seen Phosfer'? The wide, googly eyes of the nurse glared accusingly at the blank stares of several pairs of eyes. 'She just went through to the smoking room. Then she disappeared'! The ward was searched. One nurse ran out the back door and I ran out the front. She was nowhere to be seen. Nurses from other wards were enlisted to search the grounds; meanwhile, we quizzed all the nurses and porters to discover how she had managed to escape through a locked door? Nobody had come through the ward door, in the crucial ten-minute time frame. 'I must have let her out, when I let the patients out to their therapies'. I stared in disbelief, as my mouth made the confession. I was suddenly wide-awake. It was bad enough, suffering the stares of betrayal from my colleagues, but what if Phosfer managed to kill herself? How could I live with that guilt?

An hour had passed and still no sign. We were all prowling the hillside hoping to get a glimpse of her. She could be lying among the ferns and heather, unconscious and bleeding to death, or had she managed to climb a pylon and touch the high voltage lines? On our return to the ward, the doorbell rang. Probably the police, come to pick up the 'missing persons' form. They had said they would take the dog along, so we had her nightdress for the scent. It was Phosfer! 'Where the hell did you get to? We were all worried about you'. 'Just went for a walk round' she quipped nonchalantly, then strolled past us and had a smoke. At that moment, I hated the bitch, for making me look so foolish!

Minor suicide attempts continued, requiring a plaster or a stitch, with a sharp word of caution. Her husband and two young boys continued to pay the odd visit, but although she was fine with the boys, her attitude toward her husband was strained and unnatural. Other than Phosfer being cleaner and looking smarter, there was no change in her presentation. It was getting beyond a joke, that we had to allocate a nurse to special her 24/7, so it was decided, between the consultant and the charge nurse, to downgrade her observations. This meant that an allocated nurse would simply 'eyeball' her every quarter hour and tick the appropriate box in her sheet.

The allocated nurse, let Phosfer through to the dormitory to change her top. On the quarter hour, the nurse went to check on her. As she passed the glass door, leading to the clinic room, she was horrified to see a sheet of flames, through the glass. Phosfer had set her nylon blouse alight; a ball of fire sizzled on her body. Grabbing a small metal bin and filling it with water, she managed to douse the flames. The consultant reckoned it would require plastic surgery to repair her scorched abdomen. Had it not been for the quick action of the nurse, the whole hospital could have been burnt to the ground! Something had to be done! It could not go on like this indefinitely.

Two days later, I was ushered into the office to face the charge nurse and the ward consultant. The charge nurse spoke. 'You seem to have a good rapport with Phosfer, so we wondered if you would agree to take charge of her care'? This was the last thing I had expected, but was flattered by the compliment, or was it a case of, 'any port in a storm'! 'Tell you what, I'll have a word with Phosfer and if she agrees to work with me and I think it will make a difference, then ok, but I will need all the staff to cooperate with the new care plan'. The charge nurse sounded almost relieved. 'That sounds reasonable. If you think you can make a difference, then, I'll make sure the staff are behind you'.

Where to Now

It was time to move on! I had felt this need for over a year now, finally I had to leave the family home. Don't ask me why! I have no idea. Moved in with another woman got divorced and remarried; not being a genius has its pitfalls! How do you make an idiot twice as bright? Light a candle. At the time I imagined myself to be really happy, though there was a part of me that felt guilty. Should I have sacrificed the remainder of my life wondering what I had missed? The boring certainty of my old life, with the knowledge that if I hadn't made the move, then the door of opportunity would be slammed in my face. My family would suffer from a sad, grumpy individual who would feel more like a lodger?

For the first time in my life, I could spend my money on anything I wanted, not confined to a set amount each week and I had holidays abroad. It felt great and it felt right. Perhaps the difficulty was, that as the husband and wife get older, their outlook, perceptions, needs and values change in different ways and at different times! It must be a very fortunate couple, which develop with similar values or can happily accommodate each other. Am I simply rationalizing my own deficiencies, making excuses for my weak moral grounding?

We are constantly changing, in one-way or another. Moving forward, backward, up, down, even sideways. Beliefs we held as youngsters, can dissipate into silly ideas. At one time we may have loved the city life, with its noise, traffic, lights and excitement, but now crave the peaceful tranquillity of the countryside. Understanding, for mankind, is like chasing a dream! With all our accumulated knowledge, we have barely scratched the surface of a grain of sand. We must be the least enlightened animals on the planet! Constantly bickering and fighting each other, we are now even destroying our habitat, through global warming and the capacity to decimate the world with a single explosion! In truth, we will never be wiped out, because nature always finds a way to save us from ourselves! Like water finding its own level, so the balance will be found to thwart mankind's stupidity!

Becoming dissatisfied and unhappy with my life, I blamed everything around me, my home, my job, the environment, even politics? When people tell us stories, rumours, little seeds of truth, it is our reactions that encourage them to fan our smouldering fears into flaming terror! When I remarried, I thought I had finally conquered my demons, but in truth, all I was doing was placating them, dancing to their tune!

Daddies Boy.

'Ham' was due to be admitted into the ward tomorrow! As usual, he had got pissed, tried to get into a nightclub and when he was reminded that he had been banned last week, an almighty scrap ensued. He would be kept in the cells overnight, and then transferred to us on an emergency certificate, section 24 of the Mental Health Act. Now, fortunately, I had missed his three previous admissions, over the year, as I had been on holiday or relieving on another ward. I was told that every time he was admitted, he would struggle and fight with all the staff and patients; this went on for days, despite numerous injections to try and calm him down. He would have been good looking, but for the extensive bruising and swelling all over his body. When he settled down, he was a model patient, helpful and considerate to everyone. Considerable tender loving care was needed to reduce his pain, swelling and bruising.

I was asked if I would be kind enough to take charge of him, during his stay in the ward. At first I wondered if the charge nurse was simply having a laugh, but there was no smile and his fingers were crossed! Taking time out, for a cup of tea, I struggled with my dilemma. Should I be 'kind enough' to fight with this patient for days, until he settled, or simply advise the charge nurse to go and boil his head? I suppose you guessed! The second option was worse than the first, by a long chalk, so, we were stood at the rear door of the ward to receive our patient from the police van! He was in handcuffs, marched into the secure room between two seven feet by five feet officers, who then released him and vanished! The five of us looked at each other and then at 'Ham'. What now? He looked like a cross between a Japanese and a Rastafarian, with his slanting eyes and dreadlocks! I stepped forward and slapped him on his broad back. "Welcome to the ward, mate. Do you fancy a cup of tea and we can have a chat?" He looked at me, bemused. The other nurse's tensed up, ready to leap into the fray. "Yes, that would be great. Can I have a sandwich too, I'm starving!" His voice was like sandpaper. "Of course you can". One of the nurses went of to get it. "I'm your nurse, so anything you need, just ask me. We have all your details from previous visits, so just relax and enjoy your stay! With any luck, we can find out what's causing all your problems and help you deal with them. Does that sound reasonable to you?" He stood up and stretched his muscular arms. Was he about to blow? We tried not to show our fear. "I don't think that is possible, but I suppose it's worth a try".

As he supped his tea and guzzled the cheese sandwich, my mind raced to think of a way to keep the tension down. I told the other nurses to leave, first ensuring that the personal alarm radio was working! When we were alone, I sat opposite him. "Thanks for accepting your transfer to hospital, so well. I fully expected to be fighting for my life". His grin exposed white even teeth. "I'm knackered. Maybe, after a sleep I could oblige". I explained to him that he would be nursed in the single room for a few days, if he was settled after that he would join the other patients in the main ward. Shaking his hand, I said goodnight, would see him in the morning and hoped he had a good sleep.

Ham was a wonderful fellow, because, he was responsible for all the overtime that I was doing. Once he got washed and dressed, in the morning, his porridge, rolls and tea was placed on his table. He had slept soundly and when he finished his breakfast, it seemed he was ready for action! It was clear that he was unsure of what to do next and usually that meant that he had to fight! "I suspect that you do the same routine as me, in the morning!" His reply was full of menace. "What do you do in the morning?" "Well, I always do my exercises". I lied, without so much as a blush. "Here's what I do". So saying, I proceeded to do press-ups. "You probably do more than me". He could not resist the underlying challenge in my words. For the next hour, we did our macho best to outdo each other.; press-ups, sit-ups, squats, star jumps, pull-ups on the doorframe, even handstands against the wall, whilst doing press-ups! Finally, I was completely bushed and so was he, so we agreed that we would continue the next morning. "That was great. I need a doss now. I'll catch you later". He was asleep before his head hit the pillow!

I felt that we were hitting it of, because he became more talkative, speaking about his girlfriends, nights out with the boys and even how he seemed to be a magnet for a fight! Basically, if anyone gave him an order, he would attempt to tear him apart. A woman, on the other hand, could say anything to him, but he was very possessive and this usually frightened them of.

This morning we did all the usual exercises, then extra stretching and into some yoga postures, 'the cobra', 'preying mantis' and others that were variations of standard postures. Afterwards, we sat down and chatted about his friends and family, until I asked about his father! He tensed up, his hands clenched and his jaw quivered. "We never spoke about him. He disappeared when I was born; I suppose he didn't want me. Sometimes, I imagine that a man in a crowd could be him, but then, he wouldn't want to know me anyway, so what's the point. He must hate me!" The hurt in his voice was so sad. It seemed that all his problems stemmed from the belief that his father hated him. His drinking, fighting and self-hate, were all symptoms that had sprung up, to deal with his disappointment.

We talked more about his father, or at least, his theories about him, for in fact, he knew nothing about him. His mother would never speak of him and Ham didn't like to ask, in case it would cause her pain. "What do you think you father might look like? For all we know, he could be dead!" As we bounced ideas of each other, it was obvious that he had never thought beyond his bad feelings about his father; I tried to decide what the best way forward was? When in doubt, go by your instinct. "So you don't really know why your father left home! Perhaps your parents had a disagreement, or his work took him away. Maybe, he was in the forces!" His eyes opened wide, trying to assimilate this new and different father. "Actually, Ham, I'm sure that if your father could be here, the pair of you would get on like a 'house on fire'. Remember, the pair of you will have many similarities; looks, mannerisms, habits and most important, the same blood!" His body was now a picture of relaxed composure and he was trying to hide an embarrassed smile. I left him to have a sleep.

A couple of days and Ham joined the other residents in the ward; we missed out the morning exercise. He was discharged a week later, never to be readmitted. He may have move away! I hope he managed to find peace and his 'inner father'.

Kangaroo Rehab.

Phosfer had kept her head down, but we had noticed her eyeing up lighters lying on tables, empty cans in the bucket and watching the doors open and close. I asked her if we could have a word, in the clinic room, expecting her to tell me to 'piss off'! She followed me into the room, where she had burnt herself so badly a week before. We sat at the desk and I pulled my chair up beside her. 'I would like us to work together, maybe find a way to change how you are feeling and reacting'! Glaring at me, as if I had asked her to strip naked, she spoke incredulously. 'What makes you think you can possibly change the way I feel. Nothing can help, but killing myself'! Feeling pity for her desperation, I reached out to touch her hand. She withdrew her hand so fast; I got a fright. 'Sorry is your hand sore'? 'I do not like to be touched by anyone'!

We were getting nowhere, so I had to put it on the line. 'Listen Phosfer, as things stand, you can look forward to being doped up and your freedom restricted for the foreseeable future. If you can begin to trust me then we can work through your problems and break them down into manageable parts. I have tended to specialize in your illness, but the good thing is that I care and that means I will do my utmost to ease your suffering'. It looked as though she might break down and cry. 'It seems I would be crazy to turn down your offer. What do I need to do'? 'Firstly, and most importantly, you must put aside this suicide business. Give me two weeks; if you decide we are getting nowhere, we can call the whole deal off. We will measure all your symptoms and reactions, so we know where we are and when things change. Anything we talk about will stay between us, unless the others need to know, everything must be agreed between us. Do you agree'? To my amazement, she was genuinely impressed and promised to abide by the rules for 14 days. A contract was written up and we both signed it. I even managed to get her to shake hands on it! 'Nothing, and I mean Nothing, will happen without your knowledge'.

I spoke to our ward consultant Dr. brow, who was one of the few doctors that I respected. He would speak to the patients as if they really mattered, would even discuss a patient's management with a lowly nurse! 'I have managed to get phosfer to agree to play safe for two weeks' It always felt strange, that he did not interrupt. 'with that in mind, could you give her some parole? I do not think she will abuse it and it will show trust on both sides'. He was well aware of the consequences if things went wrong! But the alternative could ruin her life. He scanned her notes. 'You're taking a big chance here.' He turned over a page, in her already bulky notes. 'Your reputation is on the line here... just one minor mishap then we lock her up and throw away the key'! 'That sounds a good deal to me. Thanks'! It was time to prove that all the books I had read, classes I had attended and the theories that bounced around my skull, were worth a shit and could help our poor 'fire queen'.

It is important to observe the rules, with this type of problem. Going straight for the jugular, attacking the central issues first, would be tantamount to opening up a festering psychological bomb! Initially we have to strengthen up the ego foundations, so that the building would not collapse at the slightest tremor. Always listening to the client and at a pace the client feels comfortable with. If we go too fast, our client will flounder, in a confused, bewildered state and feeling even more unworthy! Control, is a prominent symptom that requires careful monitoring, as does respect and empathy for their suffering. At first, she was encouraged to talk about her experiences, while I listened, in a non-judgemental and non-threatening attitude.

At times, it was very hard not to show my disgust at what this pig had put her through. Some nights, he would encourage two of the kids to perform sexual acts together, so that he could get aroused. Exposing himself, they would be forced to carry out oral or vaginal stimulation on his 'tool'. Phosfer explained that because he was, so well endowed, they had great difficulty accommodating him. While Phosfer was explaining some of the intimate sexual details, I sometimes, to my horror, became aroused! She would laugh and point at my discomfort! With a red face, I would tell her that it was a normal physiological response, but our self-control and respect for others, was the line that separated us from the animals! This explanation would hopefully increase her understanding and self-worth.

A terrible dichotomy arose from the fact that, whilst she had been terrified by the excruciatingly painful vaginal penetration, a part of her needed to feel loved and wanted. So many conflicting memories would bombard her thoughts at the same time, love/hate, tenderness/ferociousness, innocence/guilt, joy and sorrow. The inability to question her thoughts, because of all these conflicts, made it impossible to resolve her problem and move on.

During our discussions, I would often reach out and touch her hand. This would gradually desensitise the problem of intimacy and allow her to feel comfortable with touch. Finally, she was able to hold her children, without having a panic attack. The longstanding issue of her flashbacks, which occurred every half hour, was the next problem we had to deal with. They were more vivid at night, so the night shift were instructed to observe when she woke up with a start. At this time, she fully believed she was back at the orphanage and even felt the same disgusting pain between her legs. The female nurse would speak to her, explaining where she was, the date and time and that she was safe. Eventually, these flashbacks would diminish, with longer periods between them, though it is unlikely that they will ever disappear!

Her husband and two girls, who were eight and nine years old, arrived on one of their rare visits. Because the father was unable to look after the boys, they stayed in a Care Home, ran by the social work. Phosfer was great with the girls, but totally ignored the father? He did not seem too bothered, would chat to the staff and patients or go out for a smoke. One day, after such a visit, Phosfer asked if she could have a word with me in private! We duly withdrew to the clinic room and sat at the desk. She started to speak a couple of times, but seemed to choke on the words; her face became mottled with red patches on her cheeks and forehead. 'It's ok, it was nothing'. She sprang up and made for the door. 'You know by now, you can speak to me about anything'. She turned and looked at me, as I spoke, her eyes moist, hand on the doorknob. 'Whatever is bothering you, will only get sorted if we can talk about it. Take a deep breath, acknowledge your heartbeat and realise it is all in the past'. Under her breath she muttered, 'bastard'! 'A year ago, just when I thought my life resembled normality, he took to drinking. That was bad enough in itself, but then he demanded we have sex, 'doggy style', saying it was the only way he could enjoy it'. She breathed deeply, and then sat on a chair. 'I began to get depressed and the flashbacks became more intense'. 'It was only because of our chats that I began to make the connection between this and my experience at the orphanage'.

Abuse victims can suffer from, Post traumatic stress disorder. Crash survivors, war veterans, sexual and physical abuse victims, are a few of the causes of this syndrome. The symptoms include, startle response, jumping when they hear a loud noise or reacting angrily, guilt regarding their behaviour at the event or even the fact that they survived, emotional coldness might be a way to avoid unwanted feelings, sleep disorders and avoidance of places or activities, the list could go on forever depending on the circumstances.

Victims can progress through several stages while in recovery. It is not uncommon for them to believe that it was their own fault or even responsibility for what happened to them! 'It was my fault because I was bad'. The perpetrator will encourage this response by saying that the victim encouraged them by showing off their body or touching them. Believing that they could have prevented the whole thing is soon dispelled when they are helped to realize how young, innocent, vulnerable and weak they were at the time of these attacks! Putting the onus onto the perpetrators by explaining their wickedness, deviousness and selfishness, all help to put it into a proper perspective. Guilt, disbelief, confusion, realisation, hurt and anger, can all occur in varying degrees. Working through this minefield, dealing sensitively with all the ramifications, will hopefully bring them to a healthy resolution! It all depends on how we cope, or don't, with our experiences.

Phosfer and I spoke about all her possible plans for the future. We even talked around the option of suicide and the consequences for her and her children! Desensitizing the flashbacks and startle responses, helped her to get a better sleep at night and in turn made her fresher and stronger, which in turn helped her deal with her numerous physical and mental symptoms? Constantly getting her to think in the present time, to be aware of her environment, attending to her personal appearance, reading daily papers and anything that would organise her thinking in a positive way, were all part of the ward program, that helped her and other clients to move forward. As she was very fit, we encouraged her to join in group games like badminton, table tennis, football and help her mingle with others and make friends. It is great to be normal. Isn't it?

Eventually, Phosfer was discharged from the hospital. She got rid of her man and had a good relationship with her children. Sure, there were setbacks, but as long as she could look back and appreciate the immense improvement in her life and the positive future, then she could handle the glitches and move forward. It was always emphasised that the successes were entirely her own achievement, all I had done was suggest what she might do, but it was her courage, integrity, intelligence and tenacity that had changed her life for the better.

Daddies Girl

Nurse Sheila blinked with the shock as the sound of the slap across her face cracked through the ward. Every face was turned to look at 'Tishy'! "Leave me alone, you stupid bitch," she screamed at the shocked nurse "it's my business if my boyfriend sleeps with me." The problem was that Tishy and her boyfriend were patients and their illicit bedtime secret had been finally uncovered.

Once the patients were all in bed tucked up and counted for the bed state form, the night-nurse seated comfortably and wrapped up in his blanket 'Tody' laid quietly and listened. He was a short, stubby lad with small round eyes and a nose that had stopped too many punches, in the numerous scraps, due to his quick, fiery temper. The chorus of deep breathing, wheezing and snoring muffled the rustle of the bedclothes as he slid clumsily out of bed. The pillows were artistically placed under the blankets to form a body shape. Why did the dormitory door seem to screech and grate so loudly despite his application of butter to the hinges that very afternoon? He listened, the chorus unchanged he closed the door behind him and tiptoed along the back corridor.

The gentle squeaking of the pinewood boards stopped when he walked at the edge. A massive oak door barred his way into the female dormitory, but it swung open noiselessly and he could see the female nurse sitting under her nightlight, knitting a jumpsuit, in pink fluffy wool, for her first grandchild. The cardigan for her son had taken more wool than expected and the baby was due any minute now. Her mind created the panic of the birth and all the tiny booties, suits and silly knickknacks that the silly relative would smother the baby in. The christening would, of course, be a solemn event, followed by her husband 'wetting the babies head', getting pissed and telling his smutty jokes which everyone had heard a dozen times. She squirmed in her seat at the embarrassment. Fortunately, Tishy slept in the corner beside the door and as he slid quietly in beside her, the warmth of her full, warm body pressing against him made his head throb, she wrapped her arms around him and smothered him in kisses. Now they could sleep, happily entwined as nature intended.

The screaming wakened the whole dormitory, even the nurse looked up from her knitting. "There's a beast attacking Tishy, nurse! Nurse!" The rhythmical squeaking, due to heightened emotions had wakened Plumy, in the next bed. The lights flicked on in time to see Tody fall out of Tishy's bed, stumbling out the door pulling up his trousers and tucking in his bits.

Tishy was carted off to the notorious locked ward, to teach her the 'pleasures' of chastity? Anything, that wasn't nailed down, was thrown at the nurses. Things settled down when she picked up a chair, "I'm leaving here, now." She hurled the chair at the window. As it bounced of the reinforced glass and frame, it spun over and clattered her on top of her head. It was a two-paracetamol job!

Over the following week, Tishy revealed herself to be kind and considerate to everyone. Always helping the less able patients, cleaning and tidying around the ward. Without warning, she would suddenly start throwing things about and when there was nothing left; she would jump onto a window ledge and begin to rip out handfuls of her beautiful blonde hair. Her pretty, young face was streaked with black mascara lines, as the tears flooded down and over her ample, naked frontage. Speaking softly, as I stroked her face, she quickly relaxed and I helped her down onto a seat. Then she really collapsed into herself, weeping and wailing, breathing in gasps as she rocked uncontrollably, "Why did he lie to me all these years?" she repeated over and over again.

She was happy. Starting school was great fun and so many people to chat with. At home, it was very strict, as an only child her mother seemed frightened of her, keeping her at arms length with lots of little chores and only speaking when giving orders. Dad ignored her completely; so it was a delightful shock when he came to her bedroom late one night. "Now that you are being educated at school, it is my duty to teach you what every woman must know". He sat tentatively on the edge of her bed and she realized that he was only wearing a dressing gown! "You must never talk about this, though it is a natural practise between father and daughter and happens in every loving family." So saying, he removed his dressing gown and slid into bed beside her. Tishy was in seventh heaven. Her father loved her and was sacrificing his time to teach her the 'art of womanhood' as every girl, with a loving father, was entitled to.

It was not until her final year at school, that she happened to mention, to her best friend, her father's habit of sleeping with her, much as you would chat about the weather, or football results. To her amazement, her friend was horrified? "But all families do it" she declared, defensively, thinking that her friend must be unloved by her family. "No they don't" her friend shouted, "I need to go, things to do. See you". In future Tishy would be more careful, when inquiring about 'the family thing'. It was smarter to make a joke of her main question, 'Does your dad teach you about the birds and bees and is he a randy beast in bed?' Amid shrieks of laughter, her fears were confirmed. It was not normal to have sex with your father. It was far from normal!

From thereon it was downhill, drink, drugs, stealing, breach of the peace, assault, etc, etc, etc. Finally, her behaviour was so unpredictable and erratic; she was formally admitted to the psychiatric hospital. Tishy was happy here; other people had worse problems than her so she felt useful, helping the disabled and elderly, comforting the depressed and disturbed. She felt silly for thinking herself to be so badly done by, when they were suffering through no fault of their own, whereas she had obviously caused her own problems. In some way she must have caused her father to do what he had done. Had she been provocative in some way? Had she said something that caused it to happen? If only he hadn't lied about it all and been more honest, maybe then it wouldn't have made her feel such an imbecile, a stupid, moronic idiot.

Tishy seemed to settle into the routine of the locked ward, trying very hard to be 'normal'. She was eating and sleeping well, working in the ward and at the recreation hall. On her transfer back to the open ward, she opted for a job with the local outpatients club. Her social worker was arranging for sheltered accommodation in the town, in preparation for her discharge. It appeared that Tishy was on the road to a full recovery.

One morning she got up early, showered, put on her make-up, pinned her hair up in a tight bun. Black brazier, pantyhose and stockings, then her short, black leather skirt was pulled up over her gaily candy stripped blouse. Finally, she slipped into her favourite high heeled, black patent leather shoes and dark brown suede jacket. Stepping prettily, out across the thin crisp layer of snow, she marched down the road, tightly clasping her small shoulder bag. Her face expressionless, mind set like granite and cold as the day, it was time! It had taken a long time to decide what she must do, but once she found the answer, it felt like she had known her fate all along.

On reaching the canal bank, she walked along to a quiet, secluded spot, where she had sat for many pensive hours in the summer. Taking off all her clothes, she folded them neatly and placed them on the bank, carefully lining up the edges and then putting her bag and her favourite shoes on top. She walked, gracefully, into the water!

As the canal contains fresh water, this, combined with the freezing temperature helps to slow down decomposition. Big boats, when they sail down through the locks, create strong currents, which drag loose debris along with it into the briny firth. Here, the corrosive salt water speeds up the breakdown of the flesh and as gasses form in the body, it finally floats and is washed up with the tide.

Abuse can take place in a host of parasitic ways. These can take the form of physical, mental, social and spiritual. Physical abuse is probably the most obvious one, including bullying, beatings and sexual abuse. Mental abuse has many twists and turns, a labyrinth of confusion, which can be so difficult to pinpoint, let alone prove. Even the perpetrators may be unaware of their crime! The constant criticism, veiled threats, put downs and silences, all feature in this abhorrent ego trip of destruction. When 'friends' berate you in front of others, ignore you in conversations or make you feel uncomfortable, then it should be considered as social abuse. Spiritual abuse hides behind a curtain of pseudo respectability, position or religious alliances. If you are not a protestant, catholic, a member, an elder or a deacon, you are made to feel like a traitor, heathen, or simply 'not one of us'.

The best way to deal with abuse is to first recognise it. This may seem a strange thing to say, but many people suffer the effects of abuse without realising that they are actually being abused. Then you must confront it! Realise that anything is better than remaining in an abusive situation. If you are unhappy, hurt, frightened or simply confused, reassess your predicament and when you realise what is wrong, get out, get a life and make things change. It takes courage to leave relationships, friends and social settings and go out into the 'great unknown', but believe me; it is never as bad or as unpleasant as the present crap! Wouldn't it be nice to be free from violence, respected, by yourself and others, listened to, be happy and spontaneous, feel like a person and have a choice?

Changes for the Better.

The care and politics of patient management, was about to be turned upside-down. Perhaps the building was considered too expensive an upkeep? Too big? Too old? Treatment policies were critically reviewed and streamlined. Their approach and efficacy were reassessed. In short, it was a cost-cutting exercise. Patients were to be dramatically reduced, by transferring them into nursing homes, back into the community, via sheltered housing, or even returned to their homes? Advertisements for 'Community Nurse Training' were all over the hospital, like an allergic rash! The remaining patients would be shifted to a brand new, modern hospital, which was being built down the road!

This also meant that staff numbers had to be reduced! This, they informed us, would be achieved by natural wastage, redundancy and retirement packages. One lad saved them the bother of his disposal; he walked into the river! The nurses were placing bets on who would stay, who would go and who else might 'top' himself? But, for some it was a golden opportunity to be given early retirement. This had to be sanctioned by the respective nursing officer, of your unit!

A number of patients bucked the system, by being unmanageable in their new 'home'! They had to be returned to the hospital, usually because they went 'high', got drunk, refused medication or assaulted a member of staff. Some surprised us all, and bets were lost, by managing to stay in their new home and even appearing happy? It was a hard time for most of us, because of the uncertainty, insecurity and confusion, which caused a massive rise in our anxiety levels. It didn't mater that the management were being so helpful and understanding, because we knew this was probably influenced by the need for our cooperation in the smooth running of the transition!

Names of staff, who wished to be considered for early retirement, had to be lodged with the personnel department. I was first in the queue. Incidents of violence, drug-induced psychosis, job dissatisfaction and the need to skive all contributed to my desire to leave. There was also the hope of setting up a business in psychotherapy! Given all these pluses, it was still a difficult call to make. Would my pension be enough to live on? I might miss the great staff that I worked with. I knew that I would miss the patients or clients, to be more politically correct! What if I failed and fell flat on my face? Could I ever return to the hospital? There were too many questions and not enough assurances! What does not kill you makes you stronger! Once again, I was unemployed!

One thing they forgot to mention; I had to be unemployed for a YEAR. My presence was requested at the job centre, once a week, on a Thursday, sign on the line, stating I had not worked since last week and I received my unemployment benefit! Then the gods shined on me! The phone rang and it turned out to be a company that ran 'Employment Assistance Programs'. His voice was smooth and syrupy, his tone crisp though pleasant. "We require a counseller in your area and I understand, from your entry in the British Association for Counselling, you possess a diploma in psychotherapy and specialize in sexual abuse trauma! Would you like to take on a case for us, in your area, we can then consider using you on a regular basis? My ship had come in! All the extra work and patience was about to pay off.

The counselling work had to remain unofficial, due to my unemployable status. Cases were few and far-between, but they were good experience and enjoyable. Finally, my year was up and I could return to official work! Anyway, my basic insecurity had long since, set in and I went to the job centre! The plum job on offer was trolley stacker, at a supermarket! The interview was more intense than the

162

one I underwent for the hospital. Over two days, the applicants filled in questionnaires and were grilled by the employment guru's. One questionnaire was by way of a psychological test and being familiar with the correct response, I happily filled it in. Some of the other forms had so many questions, I ran out of time, or was it intelligence? Anyway, I was informed that my score of one hundred percent, on the psycho, paper was enough for them to offer me the post! It was great fun, to have no responsibilities and just collect trolleys, strap them together and race them to their pen. I was warned to be careful that I did not scratch a car or run over a customer. "Not good for business, my boy!" The salary was a pittance, so after a couple of months I decided to return to nursing!

With my c.v. and passport photo, the nursing agency was happy that I had two arms, two legs and breathed. Yippee! I was an agency nurse! Hospitals, nursing homes, private homes; the variety was endless. One day it would be working in a geriatric ward, next, a young boy with tourettes, or a middle-aged woman with Alzheimer's, or a suicidal, twelve year old boy! Sometimes the job would be for months, at other times only covering a shift! You could be asked to cover a shift, with only an hour's notice. The excitement and fear, mixed with anticipation and confusion, was a heady cocktail. Once I was sent to an emergency admission unit, by mistake! It was only when I arrived, after driving for an hour through the countryside, that I discovered they needed a general nurse! It was New Years Eve; it was impossible to get a replacement. What could I do? Day staff showed me where everything was and phone numbers of doctors, if a casualty arrived! Nodding my head, at required intervals, thankfully, they did not ask any precise questions and I was left in charge of the unit, with a female auxiliary on tow? Not all was lost! On intensive questioning of the auxiliary, it transpired that she had trained up to her final year, then left, to have a baby!

The snow fell, thick and chilling. Hopefully, the weather would deter any admissions. With fingers crossed, we did a second check on the location of all the equipment, resuscitation tray, oxygen, syringes, gloves and the emergency exit? Then we sat down in front of the television and watched a repeat of a repeat, which was not very good the first time!

It was three in the morning when the phone rang, acid flushed through my brain. Attempting to sound like a general nurse, I was crisp and to the point. "Accident and emergency, how can I help you?" Fingers crossed, I prayed it was a 'wrong number'. "My fathers having a heart attack, should I bring him in?" Her gasping urgency fuelled my instincts, to put down the phone and run! "Which doctor, from the clinic, has been dealing with him?" I asked, delaying my breakdown until later. Armed with the doctor's name, I nervously rang his number. Doctor's have an intense aversion to being called out at any time, but, the early hours of New Years day, it was a brave man or a fool who would do the dirty. I was therefore amazed, when, after explaining the problem, a pleasant voice replied. "I saw the lad, yesterday. Poor sod. Tell them I will be there in a half hour. Probably needs another injection. Thanks for phoning!" After relaying the message to the relieved woman, I settled down to a soothing cup of tea. 'Perhaps I will survive the shift!' Still, my feelings of inadequacy heightened, as my gaze fell on all the equipment, pristine chrome fixtures and fittings, prepared for every eventuality. 'Alice in Wonderland' was a mere walk in the park, compared to this!

Then the unmentionable happened, we had an admission! The young man had been drinking all night and all morning. He must have thought he was a sledge? He slid down a brae, slicing his skin as he rocketed over the salt treated ice. The red sleeve on his right arm was covered in blood. Cursing and swearing, he demanded that we find his arm and sew it back on! We calmed him down by wishing him a 'Happy New Year', got him to lie on the trolley and began cleaning him up, as we contacted the duty doctor. It was then discovered that the 'sleeve', was in fact the skin hanging from his arm. Scalpel, forceps, saline solution, antiseptic lotion and bandages, were set out and the doctor cut away the loose skin. Showing the patient that he still had his arm, the wounds were cleaned and dressings applied. An almost sober, mummified patient was sent home in a taxi.

The day shift finally arrived, report given and keys handed over. Skidding home, over the ice and snow, I swore that I would never again be put in that position. Exacting questions would be asked and only jobs that I was qualified to do, would be considered! Six weeks later, the agency asked me to work at the same unit?

My disillusionment with agency nursing was further reinforced when they decided to negotiate, behind my back, to reduce my rate! It was the final straw, which pushed me into a change of employer. Information reached me that the hospital where I retired from was in dire need of 'bank' nurses. These, poor souls, are only called out when a ward was short and the full-time staff were unavailable. The sweetener was that I could do most of my shifts at night, thereby avoiding the hectic ward rounds by the doctors and the pace was more to my liking.

Attending the interview, I soon realized that there were new laws and new ideas flooding into the arena of mental nursing. It has long been a fact that nurse educational courses are pretty 'low key' with very poor incentives and even less information, as though we may be a danger if we knew what we were doing. The ward paperwork had quadrupled, which meant it was virtually impossible to complete unless you totally ignored the patients! By good luck, I was accepted and once again, I was a 'national health service' employee, I had come full circle!

I may always have a fear of being 'out of work' and 'put on the scrapheap', but the rainbow will make it seem better. All the characters that I met gave a different colour to my rainbow. The staff, patients, relatives and friends, all helped me to survive my inadequacies and fears. How some coped with insurmountable odds. Pect's blind optimism and cheerfulness. Being given a helping hand, by complete strangers, with no thought for any personal reward. My poetic father figure, so strict and yet, so kind. I could even handle the many sadness's, for they made the good times, by contrast, shine like diamonds. It has never ceased to amaze me, that what you think will happen in a given situation actually seldom does. This has led me to the conclusion that, as long as it does not harm anything or anyone, we should 'take the bull by the horns' and just go for it. We have nothing to lose but our inhibitions, false beliefs and ignorance. You might even have the best time of your life!

What Now.

Working in a number of wards, including outpatients, at the new psychiatric hospital, has been a real eye opener. The first impression that hits you is the modern open-plan layout. Every patient/client has his or her own room, a luxury I failed to foresee! They are even permitted to stay in their beds all morning, if they so wish, although this is not encouraged.

The rights of the patient/client, is paramount, with consideration given to every element of their treatment. The majority of the staff are dedicated, kind and helpful. This is amazing, given the mountain of paperwork required for each patient/client. There is also the inevitable computer records to be updated! The pace of work, by the nurses, can be quite frenetic, especially during the doctor's rounds. It is unlikely that I could function at this level, or would even wish to.

There will always be that old complaint, 'shortage of beds', from various bodies. The hospital does serve a massive area, so the turnover needs to reflect this. One aspect of this is that patients/ clients do not get a chance to hang around, as they are quickly discharged. Not much chance of, 'Institutional Neurosis'!

There are times when it is easier to think. Ideas flow, flashing pictures, memories and feelings that you can nail down and follow through to their logical conclusion. It's a real buzz when this happens, you feel so alive, self-fulfilled and worthwhile. However, at other times it's a bugger. It seems impossible to bring things to mind. What was that chaps name again? Maybe if I go through the alphabet it will remind me. It will come to me, usually when I think of something else. No ideas can be generated, feelings have no connection and I might as well have stayed in bed for the day.

Thankfully my life is now content. My partner Phyllis and I have all we need for our simple lives, together with our geriatric tomcat, Napoleon.

RAINBOWS END.

Lightning Source UK Ltd.
Milton Keynes UK
07 May 2010

153862UK00003B/67/P